ENDORSEMENTS FOR JOURNEY TO HEAVEN: A ROAD MAP FOR CATHOLIC MEN

In this book, Randy Hain gets right to the heart of what manhood is all about and how we guys can find our way in a culture that does not always value masculine virtues. With our eyes set on heaven, all our priorities in life naturally fall into place.

— Brian Caulfield —

Editor of Fathers for Good, Knights of Columbus

We have two choices: We become saints or we go to hell. There is no in-between. A saint, by definition, is someone who makes it to heaven. Randy Hain gives a very practical road map to Catholic men to help them on this journey to heaven. I encourage men to read this book and get help in their daily walk with Christ!

— Father Larry Richards —

Founder and President of The Reason for our Hope Foundation

Journey to Heaven is a book I'm thrilled to share with both of my young adults sons. Author Randy Hain does a terrific job of providing a practical, spiritually-based and tremendously engaging road map for men of all ages who desire to live a life fully devoted to God's will. You will learn from and be led by Randy's conversations with a vast cross-section of Catholic leaders. The reflection component of this book makes it the perfect choice for individual or group study.

— Lisa M. Hendey —

Founder of CatholicMom.com and Author

Mr. Randy Hain has produced for Catholic and Christian men that which the title proclaims, A Road Map, ultimately to heaven. The book is encyclopedic in its scope of suggestions and exercises for a man to live out his faith more deeply for his own spiritual benefit as well as for the Christian leadership of his family.

— Most Rev. Robert F. Vasa —
Bishop of Santa Rosa

Randy Hain has given men a clear and concise commentary on the most important aspects of our masculine lives, our ultimate goal in conforming to Christ. With his characteristically straightforward style, Randy makes a compelling case for the need men have to live a decidedly masculine pragmatic and intentional life directed both towards God and those around us. Our Lord's greatest commandment comes through in every chapter of this wonderful book along with insightful questions to compel men to think deeply about this message. I highly recommend it to men not only for reading but for action.

— Dan Spencer —
Executive Director of National Fellowship of Catholic Men

Men are often pegged as disliking road maps or directions. But, Randy Hain's engaging new book empowers men to take the reins as spiritual leaders, providers, and protectors. Hain's passion for guiding men of all ages shines through each page as he steers them clear of false idols in the culture and unambiguously points out the essential road to heaven. No matter where you are on the road map of life, this book will give you the Catholic tools, the kick in the butt and the pat on the back you need!

— Donna-Marie Cooper O'Boyle —
EWTN TV Host and Author

It is essential for every journey to know the destination and the best course to arrive there. The final sanctum is heaven but today's world does not make it easy for men to remain on the narrow path. Randy Hain has provided Catholic men with a great resource to navigate the challenges our culture presents. This book offers very sincere and concrete advice to Catholic men on integrating faith, family life, and work. Randy Hain is able to seamlessly weave the wisdom of the Church with practical insights from leading Catholic men to shed light on our pilgrimage to heaven. No Catholic man serious about being holy should leave home without this road map.

— Most Rev. Samuel J. Aquila —
Archbishop of Denver

Engaging, inspiring and full of common sense wisdom, *Journey to Heaven* should be required reading for every Catholic husband, father, brother and son. It will spark discussion, ignite imaginations—and probably lead more than a few men out of the wilderness and into a deeper life of prayer. Prepare to be challenged—and to have your life changed. Randy Hain has given us all a great gift.

— Greg Kandra —
Deacon in the Diocese of Brooklyn, Veteran Broadcast Journalist,
Multimedia Editor of Catholic Near East Welfare Association
(CNEWA), and former Writer and Producer for CBS News

Randy Hain pulls no punches. *Journey to Heaven* is an in-your-face, no-holds-barred clarion call and crystal clear road map for Catholic men to quit being wishy-washy and to courageously step up to the challenge God has given us of getting ourselves and our families to heaven.

— Greg Willits —
Director of Evangelization and Family Life Ministries
for the Archdiocese of Denver, Blogger, Podcaster, and Author

If all you do is read the chapter on Saint Joseph, you'll be a better man for it. But read the rest, so you'll be a much better man. Your family will benefit from the difference this book makes.

— Mike Aquilina —

Executive Vice-President of St. Paul Center for Biblical Theology and Author

First let me begin with a heartfelt thank you! What a wonderful book. Talk about divine intervention, as I needed a good book to read for Lent. I was amazed at the depth of Randy Hain's Catholic faith and knowledge, especially for someone who only came to the Church less than ten years ago! This book is a must read for ALL Catholic men. Cradle Catholics, RCIA Catholics and Catechumens alike. A manly reminder that being a man is not to be frowned upon or taken lightly. It is to be embraced and portrayed!

— Doug Berry —

Founder and Director of RADIX, Performer, and Co-host of EWTN's Life on the Rock

As with his other works, *Journey to Heaven* continues Randy Hain's conversational style he has honed in his speaking and writing opportunities. Focusing on the call for men to be leaders of their families, this new work outlines how the challenge of totally embracing our Catholic faith can make dynamic differences in our lives and in the lives of our families. Sharing the knowledge of so many Catholic men who he has worked with over the past years, this new book shows the beauty of life lived to the fullness in the Catholic Church and offers us men the opportunity to be iron for each other that we may support each other in the challenge to be dynamically Catholic.

— Father Kyle Schnippel —

Director of Vocations for the Archdiocese of Cincinnati

We all want to be better men! Facing the myriad of daily demands and challenges that weigh upon as leaders, fathers and husbands, it is difficult to focus on what we can do to be better. It is easy to grow weary with the immensity of our daily responsibilities. In Randy Hain's excellent and powerful new book *Journey to Heaven*, he not only encourages us, he arms us with knowledge, hope and the plan that Christ provides for each of us. Through examples from Scripture, the saints and personal experience Randy offers the modern Catholic man guidance, brotherhood and strength for the journey. In *Journey to Heaven* we see the vocation given to us by God Himself come alive and something truly amazing happens. In the process of reading this book, as you seek solutions for increasing holiness and managing your own life, one comes to understand that the struggle IS the mission. God's love for us is manifested in the burdens of our daily lives. In our personal call to holiness, through caring for wives, children, employees, coworkers and friends, we find God! His burdens become His blessing!

— Joe O'Farrell —
Vice President for Mission Advancement,
EWTN Global Catholic Network

Journey to Heaven: A Road Map For Catholic Men is a powerful and practical guide for the man who recognizes that he was meant to live for more than the paltry and shallow call of our culture. If you are looking for answers about how to be the man that God has called you to be, you won't find a better resource than this.

— Dan Burke —
Author of *Navigating the Interior Life*,
Executive Director of the National Catholic Register, and
President of the Avila Institute for Spiritual Formation

Blessed John Henry Newman wrote, "God has created me to do him some definite service. . . . I have a part in a great work; I am a link in a chain, a bond of connection between persons." This is true for each of us. In *Journey to Heaven*, Randy Hain offers encouragement and very practical lessons to help Catholic men discover a deep life of faith and live out their vocations responsibly and fruitfully as husbands and fathers.

— Mike Bickerstaff —

Deacon for the Archdiocese of Atlanta and

Editor-in-chief of The Integrated Catholic Life

In *Journey to Heaven*, Randy Hain has channeled some of the brightest and best conversation on what it means to be a man. This book isn't just for men, though. It should be part of every wife, sister, and mother's required reading, and a topic of discussion for all of us. Thank you, Randy, for baring yourself and sharing the points I want the men in my life to live.

— Sarah Reinhard —

Blogger at SnoringScholar.com and Author

Timely and dare I say necessary as we contemplate how to guide our children for the future and provide them a model for what it means to be a faithful Catholic man, husband, and father.

— Marcus Grodi —

Founder and President of

The Coming Home Network International

Journey to Heaven

A Road Map for Catholic Men

Journey to Heaven

A Road Map for Catholic Men

RANDY HAIN

Foreword by Patrick Madrid

Steubenville, Ohio
A Division of Catholics United for the Faith
www.emmausroad.org

Emmaus Road Publishing
827 North Fourth Street
Steubenville, Ohio 43952

Printed in the United States of America
19 18 17 16 15 14 1 2 3 4 5 6

Library of Congress Control Number: 2014937458
ISBN: 978-1-940329-82-6

Text design and layout by Julie Davis, General Glyphics, Inc., Dallas, Texas
Cover design and layout: Theresa Westling
Cover photo: Monica Lahr, Monica Lynn Photography

FOR ALEX AND RYAN

TABLE OF CONTENTS

PART III: WORK AND THE PUBLIC SQUARE

APPENDICES

Foreword

Consider the old adage:

Sow a thought, reap an act.
Sow an act, reap a habit.
Sow a habit, reap a character.
Sow a character, reap a destiny.

Each moment of each hour of each day, whether you realize it or not, whether you *intend* it or not, you are forming habits that shape your character and will eventually determine whether you will spend eternity in heaven or hell. When this earthly life ends and you pass from time into eternity, it will be too late to change your mind and thus change your destiny.

Now is the time to make that choice. This life is analogous to freshly poured cement that is still wet and malleable; you still have time to discard bad habits, acquire good ones and, by God's grace, form your character for the good, ordering your love and life toward God and the things of God. Once this life is over—a moment that arrives suddenly and without warning for many people—that opportunity will have passed you by. Once the cement has hardened and set, it can no longer be molded and shaped.

It is 100 percent in your best interests to act *now*. You can't lose if you do so. God will help you with everything you need to complete this mission.

Take stock of your situation. If you are wallowing in chronic sin, repent and turn away from anything that you know is incompatible with your Christian beliefs and keeps you apart from God who loves you. If you are lukewarm, then get fired up! Jesus warns in Revelation 3:16 about what will happen to those who live in the mushy middle and are neither hot nor cold. If you are on the right track and know you are making some progress but still see areas of your life that are weak, wobbly, and not properly squared away, then take action now to correct those problems. The Lord is waiting to help you with His grace. So ask Him to.

Hebrews 9:27 reminds us, *[I]t is appointed to a man to die once, and then the judgment.* And in 2 Corinthians 6:2 St. Paul says, *Behold, now is the acceptable time; behold, now is the day of salvation.*

Don't put it off.

If heaven is where you want to spend eternity, then you must act now, decisively choosing to spend the rest of your life striving for that one, all-important goal that Jesus describes as loving God with all your heart, mind, and strength.

But how to do that? In particular, how to do that in the midst of the hectic demands, busy schedules, and ubiquitous interruptions with which the modern world surrounds us?

You know all too well how distracting, disconcerting, and disorienting daily life can be.

The world says, "There's an app for that." Well, Jesus says, "There's a grace for that." And not just "grace" in an abstract, nebulous sense, but real, hardcore, armor-piercing grace that comes to you in and through the sacraments of the Church He established, especially the Holy Eucharist and Confession, as well as the Holy Bible, prayer, and good works done in grace, what St. Paul describes as "faith working through love" (Galatians 5:6). These are the surefire, divinely instituted "apps" for the Christian life. So use them!

God knows exactly what you need as a man, not just to cope with life's preoccupations but to overcome them, to conquer them, and to begin thriving as a Christian man who has determined at all costs to put truth and goodness, beauty and integrity first, before all else.

Men are physiologically, mentally, and emotionally external and projecting. That's why we like contact sports. We instinctively seek to act upon things. Collisions, building, fixing, defending, and struggling with the world around us are all natural and legitimate aspects of our God-designed masculinity. The Lord wants us to live out our masculinity in its fullness, each in our own way and according to the particular talents, temperaments, and circumstances He has given us.

Women are physiologically and emotionally internal and receptive. They complement, civilize, and complete us men (thank God!) with their marvelous feminine gifts for receiving, gathering, and nurturing.

To grow into spiritual and emotional maturity, we men need something outside ourselves to show us that we have passed the tests for becoming real men. Most fundamentally, we need affirmation that our actions are valued and important, that we are in fact accomplishing the mission undertaken.

At Jesus' baptism, God the Father's voice boomed from heaven declaring: *This is my beloved Son in whom I am well pleased*. Boys need to hear that from their dads, husbands need to hear the equivalent from their wives. Most of all, though, men need to hear that message from the Lord. And the only way that will happen is through "turning away from childish things" and becoming the man God is calling you to be.

This book presents a great many important truths, reminders, lessons, and encouragements for how you can begin today—right here, right now—becoming that man the Lord wants to make you. Randy Hain has performed a vital service to men everywhere who take to heart and implement the sound instruction and proven advice he shares in *Journey to Heaven*.

— Patrick Madrid, January 2014 —

Acknowledgements

When I am finishing a new book I always enjoy writing the acknowledgements, as it gives me an opportunity to reflect on the wonderful people who have been part of making the book project come to life. I am grateful to Mike Sullivan and Shannon Hughes of Emmaus Road Publishing for their enthusiasm and support for *Journey to Heaven*. It makes the author's job much easier to know the publisher is fully behind you!

Patrick Madrid wrote the excellent Foreword for the book and I can't thank him enough for his contribution and the incredible ministry he offers the Catholic world through his books and speaking. Patrick is a blessing to the Church. In the spirit of this project I thank him as my brother in Christ.

Gail Coniglio has been a tremendous help as my literary agent, encourager in chief, and friend to make *Journey to Heaven* come to life. I can always count on Gail for sage advice, enthusiastic support, and prayers. I also appreciate that she never hesitates to tell me the truth.

Thank you Dr. Bill Thierfelder, Bishop Michael Sheridan, Matt Swaim, Matt Warner, Peter Herbeck, Tom Peterson, Father Dan Ketter, Father Martin Connor LC, Deacon Mike Bickerstaff, Rick Swygman, Andy Mangione, Dr. Rob Kaiser, Kevin Lowry, Joel Schmidt, Dan Burke, Brian Caulfield, Ken Davidson, Father Kyle Schnippel, Chris Stefanick, and Patrick Trueman for the candid and heartfelt insights you shared throughout *Journey to Heaven*. The great example you provide to other Catholic men through the testimony of your lives is inspiring and this is a better book because you selflessly offered your help. I will always be grateful to you.

To the men of WBC Atlanta, thank you for teaching me the necessity and value of brotherhood. I don't say it enough, but your support, prayers, candor, and friendships mean a great deal to me.

To the countless Catholic men I have met around the country since joining the Church, I am appreciative of the time you have spent with me sharing your challenges, worries, triumphs, and blessings. Much of what you read in *Journey to Heaven* was influenced by our conversations.

Monsignor Peter Rau, thank you for the blessing and prayers you offered at a critical juncture to help me complete *Journey to Heaven*. That was the spiritual shot in the arm I needed to complete the book.

My father Steve Hain is my role model and much of the practical wisdom he has shared with me over the years has influenced what you will read in this book. Thank you, Dad.

I am blessed to have a loving and supportive family who encourage me and keep me focused on what is important in life. Thank you, Sandra, Alex, and Ryan.

St. Joseph, Patron Saint of Fathers, please know I am grateful for the example you set which is the model for all Catholic men. Please pray for us, that we may courageously live up to our calling, pursue lives of holiness, and attain heaven.

Introduction

"Why did you write this book?" a friend asked me not long ago. The answer should have been simple: I am a Catholic man and I wanted to write a practical and helpful book for other Catholic men who face the same issues I do in their daily lives. But, the answer is deeper and more complex. I felt drawn to this topic because I am greatly troubled by the world in which we live. I am concerned that our young people, especially young Catholic men, are growing up without understanding their faith, their God-given responsibilities as men, and are being led astray by the false idols of our modern culture.

Men in general are faced with significant challenges. The feminization of masculinity is a well-documented and growing trend. Man's role as head of the family is under attack and pornography is devouring men of all ages at an alarming rate. So, you might ask, why not write a book about all men and not just Catholic men? The response is that Catholic men have added responsibilities and obligations which set them apart. As Catholics, we know we are made for heaven and not this world.

As Catholics, we know we are called to be saints and to lead lives of holiness. As Catholic men, we know our vocation is to help our families get to heaven.

So, as Catholic men, we better know—precisely—what it entails to "get to heaven." We better know the significance and real consequences of Jesus Christ's admonition recorded in Matthew 25:31–47: *When the Son of Man comes . . . he will sit on his glorious throne . . . he will separate them one from another . . . and they will go away into eternal punishment, but the righteous into eternal life*. I have found that it always helps to begin any task with the ultimate end in mind. And I can't think of a better motivation for practicing our Catholic faith than the mental image of Jesus greeting us in heaven with the words, *Well done, good and faithful servant* (Matthew 25:23).

In our heavenly Father, in St. Joseph, in countless other saints, and in a few courageous men of today we have excellent role models to follow. The Bible and Catechism of the Catholic Church offer us well-defined teaching, and the Church gives us access to the sacramental life. We know what we are supposed to do and have all the resources we need, yet many of us are still struggling.

Out of a desire not only to help and encourage the Catholic men of today but also to leave a useful resource and road map for future generations, I humbly offer you *Journey to Heaven: A Road Map for Catholic Men*. This is not a book heavy in Catholic theology, but everything it contains is consistent with and drawn from Church teaching. This is not a book about theories, but a practical book filled with candor and practical action with contributions from inspiring Catholic men who have shared their insights and experiences.

Journey to Heaven is divided into three sections: Faith, Family, and Work and the Public Square. The book addresses topics such as pride, prayer, the Eucharist and Reconciliation, friendship, marriage, courage, fatherhood, integrating faith and work, setting priorities and leading by example. There is even a chapter on how Catholic men of today can be rebels—in a positive way! There are also three Appendices dealing with (1) the ruinous impact of pornography; (2) the call to the priesthood, diaconate, and religious life; and (3) helpful resources for Catholic men. Regardless of age or marital status, I pray every Catholic man will find value in reading the book.

Guys, we are here to do more than sit on the sidelines. We are called to lead and set a good example. We are called to lead our families and help them get to heaven, get involved in our parishes, give back to our communities, and have a positive influence on our friends and those we encounter each day. I pray that this book is helpful to you and the Holy Spirit will use it to bring about whatever changes are necessary to get on the right path and embrace our Catholic manhood, and help us teach future generations to do the same.

We are all made for heaven. Let's act accordingly!

AUTHOR'S NOTE

Because of the action-oriented focus of this book, I encourage you to take notes in a notebook or journal as you read it. Each chapter has questions for reflection which will likely generate thoughts, ideas, and specific actions you will not want to forget. This book is ideal for either individual reading or as a book for study in a Catholic men's group.

PART I

FAITH

CHAPTER ONE

What are the Obstacles Between Us and Christ?

Isn't it tough to go it alone?
Seriously, how effective are we if we only
rely on ourselves for the answers.
— Author —

As long as we live in the world our life is a constant struggle between love for Christ or giving into lukewarmness, to our passions, or to comfort seeking, which destroys love. Faithfulness to Christ is forged each day by struggling against what separates us from him, and by an effort to make progress in virtue. Then they will be faithful both when times are good and when they are difficult, when it seems few remain by Our Lord's side.
— Francis Fernandez —

I recall a conversation with a Catholic friend over lunch some time ago about the obstacles between men and Christ. After the usual story swapping and a discussion about bad cultural influences, my friend left the table saying, "I need to get back to the office. Next time we get together we should brainstorm a handy checklist for Catholic men so we won't forget what we are supposed to be doing!" The conversation stuck with me and the checklist idea eventually became this chapter.

As I pondered the obstacles keeping me from Christ, and those shared by other Catholic men I have encountered over the years since my conversion into the Church, it was very convicting and challenging as I was reminded of where I continually fall short. Yet, reflecting on this list has also inspired me and I try to reflect on how to overcome these obstacles during my daily prayer time. I have a long way to go, but I believe that greater awareness of these obstacles and a determined focus on overcoming them will bring me closer to Christ and my desire to attain heaven.

Before I share some of the common obstacles between us and Christ, let's consider what we know for certain. We have a goal (to get to heaven and to avoid hell), a road map (Scripture and Tradition), examples to follow (the saints, particularly St. Joseph), leadership (the pope, bishops, priests, and deacons), clear teaching authority (the magisterium of the Church), help along the way (the sacraments) and divine guidance (the Holy Spirit). It is clear that we are well equipped and have the tools and resources we need, but are we willing to make the necessary changes?

OBSTACLES BETWEEN CATHOLIC MEN AND CHRIST ... AND ACTIONS TO OVERCOME THEM

PRIDE

We have to surrender on an ongoing basis to Christ for His will to be done in our lives. He is not looking for a copilot. He is the pilot. Guys, we simply have to recognize that we are not in charge—as much as we want to be! The next chapter deals with pride and surrender in greater detail.

WE DON'T FULLY APPRECIATE THE EUCHARIST

All of us have an opportunity every single day to have the most personal relationship possible with Christ by partaking of the Eucharist during Mass, yet we may not truly understand or appreciate this great gift He has given us. Many parishes offer Eucharistic Adoration, which provides an opportunity to kneel and pray before the True Presence of Christ in the Blessed Sacrament. We will never know Him if we don't spend time with Him.

LACK OF A PRAYER LIFE

We can't have a relationship with Jesus if we never talk to Him. Work on developing a daily prayer routine with the goal of at least an hour a day devoted to prayer. Sound difficult? Think about how much TV we watch a day. Consider how much time we spend in our cars each day and how much time we devote to exercise. We have more than enough time for prayer if we plan for it, schedule it, and commit to it. Pray the Morning Offering or other prayers before you leave home (ten minutes), five decades of the Rosary in your car or while exercising (twenty minutes), the Daily Jesuit Examen (fifteen minutes), Grace with all meals (five minutes), and with your children and spouse (ten minutes). Add it up, and we just did an hour of prayer. (See chapter four on Prayer and appendix three for Resources.)

MISUNDERSTANDING OUR TRUE VOCATION

For those of us blessed to be married and have children, we must recognize that helping our families get to heaven and being good husbands and fathers (and not our business careers) is our real vocation. It is so easy to allow our family to serve our work (my issue many years ago) instead of having our work serve our family, and, in turn, our family to serve the Lord.

LACK OF COURAGE

If we don't acknowledge Christ, defend Him in public, and tell others about Him, we will find it challenging to be close to Him. Christians are meant to stand out, not blend in. We live in difficult, trying times. Families are under attack, our children are at risk, many people are blind to the need to respect and value all life, and atheists are one of the fastest growing groups in the world. We have an opportunity to be beacons of light and good examples of Christ's redeeming love. We will be judged one day on the fruits of our apostolate, and hope one day to hear Jesus say the words, "Well done, good and faithful servant."

LACK OF DETACHMENT

Guys, let's ask ourselves if we need "it," whatever "it" is. Does "my team" losing a game ruin my day? Do I treat playing golf, going to the gym, detailing my car as though they were more important than my family or my relationship with God who loves and created me and who is my ultimate end? If I already have a 50-inch flat screen TV, do I really need a 60-inch? If

I already have a $40,000 car, do I *really need* a $50,000 car? Am I "majoring in the miners"? Let go of the things that are in the way of our prayer lives, Mass attendance, charitable giving, volunteering, time with our families, and certainly our relationships with Christ. "An effective detachment from everything we have and are is necessary if we are to follow Jesus, if we are to open our hearts to our Lord, who is passing by and calls out to us. On the other hand, attachment to earthly things closes our doors to Christ and closes the doors to love and to any possibility of understanding what is most essential in our lives" (Francis Fernandez, *In Conversation with God,* 7-volume set, Scepter Pubs, 1993). Healthy detachment includes letting go of the opinions of others and doing what we know to be right in the face of criticism and judgment from our peers.

PORNOGRAPHY

Appendix two deals with this issue at length, but men have to guard against the increasing danger and addictive allure of pornography. What may start out as the "lust of the eyes" may turn to more dangerous forms of this epidemic. This sinful and harmful addiction is increasingly separating our men from the love of Christ. "Deep within yourself, listen to your conscience which calls you to be pure ...a home is not warmed by the fire of pleasure which burns quickly like a pile of withered grass. Passing encounters are only a caricature of love; they injure hearts and mock God's plan" (St. Pope John Paul II).

LUKEWARMNESS

As long as we live in the world our life is a constant struggle between love for Christ or giving into lukewarmness, to our passions, or to comfort seeking, which destroys love. Faithfulness to Christ is forged each day by struggling against what separates us from Him, and by an effort to make progress in virtue. Then they will be faithful both when times are good and when they are difficult, when it seems few remain by Our Lord's side" (Francis Fernandez, *In Conversation with God*, Vol. 2, 418).

DIMINISHED MANHOOD

The feminization of our culture is emasculating our manhood. Women play a very special role in the world, but so do men—and we are forgetting what God has made us to be. The surrounding culture has been lying to us about our roles for decades and we are increasingly afraid to be spiritual leaders in our own homes. We are not like women and women are not like us. Men are made in the image of God the Father and only we can emulate Him in this regard and live out our calling.

WHAT ARE THE FRUITS OF A LIFE IN CHRIST?

"Let your door stand open to receive Him, unlock your soul to Him, offer Him a welcome in your mind, and then you will see the riches of simplicity, the treasures of peace, the joy of grace. Throw wide the gate of your heart, stand before the sun of the everlasting light" (St. Ambrose).

Isn't it tough to go it alone? Seriously, how effective are we if we only rely on ourselves for the answers? I don't know about you, but I tried that way for over twenty years and it was very difficult. Having experienced a life where Christ is in charge, I have seen the other side and pray that I never have to fly solo again! Please consider your answers (as I have many times) to these important questions:

- Do I want to be a better husband to my wife?

- Do I want to be a better father to my children?
- Do I desire a stronger faith journey in the Catholic Church?
- Do I want to be a better son to my parents?
- Do I want to be a better friend? Can I be more involved in the community and helping others?
- Do I want to be a better leader at work?

As we ponder the questions above, it is probably safe to assume we said yes to each one. Now, think about surrendering yourself to Jesus and asking Him for help. We know what it is like to go it alone and if we are honest with ourselves, the results are not that great.

Giving ourselves to Him, letting our old selves go and placing Him first will change everything. We will receive His grace, guidance, and love, which in turn will positively affect our relationships with our wives, children, friends, and coworkers. We will see our faith journeys catch fire as we begin to appreciate the truth and beauty of our Catholic faith. Our appreciation of the Mass will grow exponentially as we more fully understand the gift of receiving the True Presence of Christ in the Eucharist and we are joined in intimate union with Him. We will be perceived differently as people begin to see Christ at work in us. Or we can continue to stubbornly go it alone.

Jesus Christ died on the Cross for us. He redeemed our sins. He loves us unconditionally. The only way to heaven is through Him. What does He want in return? He simply asks for ALL of us—mind, body, and soul. He wants us to place Him *first* in our lives, before family, friends, work—*everything*. Think about the list of questions above and place "Christ inspired" in front of father, husband, son, friend, and leader. How can this not be desirable?

A few years ago I was blessed to be a speaker at the Rocky Mountain Catholic Men's Conference in Boulder, Colorado. One of the other speakers who made a great impression on me was Chris Stefanick. Archbishop Charles Chaput has called Chris Stefanick "one of the most engaging young defenders of the Christian faith on the scene today." Chris speaks to over fifty thousand teens, young adults, and parents every year and has become a regular in Catholic media, appearing frequently on Relevant Radio and his videos featured on EWTN and Salt & Light (Catholic TV).

This fourteen-year youth ministry veteran served at a parish in the East Los Angeles area, as director of Youth and Young Adult Ministry for the Diocese of Lacrosse, and as director of Youth, Young Adult and Campus Ministry for the Archdiocese of Denver. He is currently founder and president of Real Life Catholic—a nonprofit organization dedicated to reengaging a generation.

One of the things I appreciate most about Chris is how proud he is to be a husband and father to six beautiful children. I was eager to get his thoughts on the obstacles between men and Christ.

Chris, I know you have been involved in Catholic young adult and Catholic men's ministries for several years. From your perspective, what are the obstacles between Catholic men and a deeper relationship with Christ?

> "To come to God deeply and authentically you have to come as you are. Openly. Honestly. Wholeheartedly.

But if men don't know who they are, how can they come to God this way?

"I think there's a cultural crisis in masculine identity. What does it mean to be a man?

"The identity gap is being filled with lies from a culture that encourages men to define themselves in all the wrong ways (money, sexual prowess, power), or that sees them as dumb oxen because they're men and happen to have twenty times more testosterone in their bodies than women.

"What's the solution? Men need other men.

"Women can affirm our masculinity, but as a very wise man once told me, only other men can confer it on us. We need brotherhood. Deep, authentic, and honest to the point of being raw. If we have that I think we can rediscover what it means to be a man, and I think we can learn, gradually, to come to God as we are.

"I have brothers in Christ in my life like this, and it's one of the greatest blessings of my life. I don't spend enough time with them, but sharing my thoughts with you reminds me that I need to."

Having heard you speak at the Colorado Springs Catholic Men's Conference a few years ago, I remember your wakeup call to Catholic men everywhere to "man up" and accept our responsibilities. What are the important responsibilities of Catholic men? Do you think the men you encounter are aware of them?

"The popes have written extensively to women in recent times. Perhaps they're compensating for the fact that women can't become priests, so it's important for the Church amidst accusations of sexism to highlight the inherent beauty of what St. Pope John Paul II called 'the feminine genius.' And that's wonderful. But I think they're forgetting that 99.9 percent (more or less) of us Catholic men aren't priests either. Which leaves me with the question, where's our apostolic letter?

"Men have been endowed by God with a special way of imaging Him to the world. Married or not, parent or not, we're all fathers at heart. We image God the Father in a way women cannot.

"I think we have refrained from reflecting on that for fear of sounding chauvinistic. Enough is enough. The sexual revolution is over. Women have the right to work and to use their gifts in any profession they want. They have the right to be bosses at any company they want. They have a place in the Church's mission and ministry (and at any given parish it's often a very important place) and I'd defend those rights. But now that that's been established, it's time to look, without fear, timidity, or apology, at the special charisms and calling we have as men!

"We are created to be spiritual leaders, providers, and protectors in a way that women are not. It seems that in the average family we have surrendered those roles to women to the point where we're MIA. Women outnumber men in the Catholic Church every Sunday by 25 percent.

"Men have to take the reins and call their families to prayer. We need to be protectors and to reflect on the spiritual trajectory of our families, of each of our children, of our spouses, and we need to shepherd them in the right direction. I'm not sure we can expect to enter the kingdom if any of our children are left behind and we didn't do anything about it, or even stop to notice what was happening as they wandered quietly into the kingdom of darkness.

"We need to be involved in the parish, in schools, in the community. And I'm not just speaking to married men, but all men, who are all called to spiritual fatherhood in their own way.

"Women are the glue of community life, and that's beautiful, if it flows from their particular gifts and charisms. But I think more often than not it also flows from the fact that men are absent from all but their jobs and the NFL."

When a Catholic man fails to address the issues you have identified, what is the impact on his marriage (or future marriage if currently single)?

"When a man doesn't know who he is, he doesn't know what he's called to bring into a marriage. He approaches marriage as a 'taker' instead. He doesn't approach it as a man, but as a baby, looking for a new source of milk to suckle. That's not what you find in marriage, and it's clearly not what the Lord calls us to in Ephesians 5: *Husbands, love your wives, as Christ loved the Church and gave himself up for her, that he might sanctify her.*

"A brother in Christ once told me that if you approached marriage seeing your wife as a balm for your wounds, which she is in some ways, you'll be shocked to see that God has planned for her also to serve as the finger of the doctor poking at and diagnosing your wounds. When you come in with a broken arm the first thing the doc does is poke your arm, 'Does this hurt?' 'Ouch! Yes!' 'Good, now we both know where you're broken and we can start to work on that.'"

If you had one chance to address an audience of Catholic men of all ages genuinely seeking to grow in their faith and accept their God-given responsibilities, what would be your message to them?

"You have twenty times more testosterone than women. That doesn't make you fallen. It's one of the many things that makes you a man. There's a reason why every nation on earth was founded by a man: testosterone! It's also why most prison inmates are probably men.

"You're more 'in the mood' than women. You're often more prone to anger than women, too. Men often think of themselves as inherently spiritually inferior to women because of those tendencies. Being a Christian man isn't about crushing all that, but

> guiding it. There's a team of horses inside of you. A life of virtue is just about making sure they pull your life in a mighty and positive direction rather than off a cliff somewhere. It's not about killing those horses.
>
> "Purity and patience aren't about never feeling aroused or angry. God wants to encourage you to rise up and become the son, brother, and father He made you to be in His image.
>
> "I'm just pointing out two particular issues, but the real issue is that when God looks at you, He doesn't see something weak and broken or dirty. He sees His son. And when He calls you, He's not calling you to become less of a man so that you can be redeemed. He's calling you to be *the man* He created you to be. He desires to nurture the best out of you."

As you ponder this chapter and the questions below, what are the barriers between you and Christ today? Do you recognize the obstacles and, most importantly, are you prepared to overcome them? The obstacles given and the actions to overcome them may seem daunting and a lot of hard work, but the real challenge is to practice these actions not as a bunch of items on a "to-do list," but as part of a broader, unifying approach to living that places Christ first in every area of our lives.

As you read the rest of this book, you will find these challenges explored in greater detail with practical actions, Church teaching and guidance from other men on how we can faithfully pursue lives of holiness and the goal of heaven.

QUESTIONS FOR REFLECTION

1. As I reflect on what I have read from the author and Chris Stefanick, are there obstacles not identified which are an issue for me in my relationship with Christ?
2. Is it painful for me to admit the presence of these obstacles in my life or do I feel more encouraged than ever to overcome them?
3. The author identified "lukewarmness" as an obstacle. Have I considered this before? Am I guilty of going through the motions with the practice of my Catholic faith?
4. If I am honest with myself, does the first obstacle of pride impede my spiritual growth and relationship with Christ much of the time? Can I identify specific times over the last several weeks when this was an easily identifiable issue? What would I do differently if faced with the same situations again?

CHAPTER TWO

Surrender!

Few souls understand what God would accomplish in them
if they were to abandon themselves unreservedly to Him and
if they were to allow His grace to mold them accordingly.
— St. Ignatius of Loyola —

Men, do we struggle with the idea of surrender? So many men I encounter were raised from an early age, like me, to be tough, to be strong, not to cry, not to show emotion. We learned to develop barriers around our hearts that keep the world at an emotional distance. The most important casualty, however, is our relationship with the Lord as we often wind up keeping Christ at a distance as well.

It is ironic that this formidable obstacle which keeps us from Christ requires what is quite possibly the hardest thing for men to do: totally surrendering to His will. One of the key obstacles to surrendering is *pride*, and we have this in abundance! The cure is *humility*, the best counter to this sin of pride. Author Peter Kreeft wrote, "Pride does not mean an exaggerated opinion of your own worth; that is vanity. Pride means playing God, demanding to be God. 'Better to reign in hell than serve in heaven,' says Satan, justifying his rebellion, in Milton's 'Paradise Lost.' That is the formula for pride. Pride is the total 'my will be done.' Humility is 'thy will be done.' Humility is focused on God, not self. Humility is not an exaggeratedly low opinion of yourself. Humility is self-forgetfulness. A humble man never tells you how bad he is. He's too busy thinking about you to talk about himself."

In many cases I would suggest that these moments of pride are what keep us from surrendering to God on a daily basis and eventually make us fearful of that surrender. I routinely observe Catholic men who come right up against a deeper faith and a closer relationship with Christ, only to walk away because of the need to surrender. Why? After countless conversations with a number of my Catholic brothers, I'd like to share some observations (and a few confidential direct quotes) on the challenges in the way of trustful surrender to our Lord:

- Surrendering/submitting to Christ and His divine will is frightening.
- Giving up control/not being in charge is scary.
- "How will my friends and peers judge me?"
- "It is tough to be vulnerable."
- There is fear of losing personal freedom.
- There is fear that the cost of surrender will be too great.
- Pride and ego always get in the way.
- Men struggle with emotional connections.

- There is a barrier around the heart, formed at a young age (my personal experience).
- "I was raised to keep this stuff inside, like my dad."
- "Work and family stress is hard enough. I don't have time for this right now."
- "I go to Mass every Sunday. Isn't that enough?"

Did any of these obstacles resonate with you? They all clicked with me. Keep these obstacles in mind as you continue reading.

To give ourselves in daily surrender to Christ, it is important to put our absolute trust in Him. What have we got to lose? When we give ourselves up, God lets Himself in, and that is exactly what He did for me. It all comes down to control versus surrender. "If we let Christ into our lives, we lose nothing, nothing, absolutely nothing of what makes life free, beautiful and great. No! Only in this friendship are the doors of life opened wide. Only in this friendship is the great potential of human existence truly revealed" (Pope Emeritus Benedict XVI, Homily of April 24, 2005).

I remember very well what my life was like before surrendering to the Lord and putting Him first in my life. All I had was family and work prior to that point, and I was in charge (I thought) of my own destiny. I dealt with life's challenges as they came and pridefully took the credit when things were going well. I thought I was being the strong husband and father that *my* father had been when I was growing up. I thought I was in control. But God had other plans for me, and as St. Bernard of Clairvaux said centuries ago, "He who is his own master is a scholar under a fool."

In the second Mass I ever attended in October 2005, shortly after my wife and I made the decision to convert and join the Catholic Church, I went through a powerful personal conversion. I was trembling, sweating, nervous, and felt weak at the beginning of the Mass. My family thought I was having a heart attack! This strange feeling lasted for about ten minutes until it passed. What happened in these few precious minutes was life altering for me. I went into the church that morning feeling lost. I knew I needed help and that I no longer had the answers. I remember praying silently to God to lead me and acknowledged that I was no longer in charge. I was feeling so weak because I had never asked God for anything before and I didn't know how to relinquish control. When I prayed those words, gave up control and sincerely surrendered to His will, I felt a surge of strength and a sense of peace that felt like a wind blowing right through me. I had given up over twenty years of stubbornness, ego, and pride that had been accumulating since I last attended the Baptist church as a teenager.

Your experience may be quite different from mine. All I can share with you is when I put my pride aside and humbly surrendered to His will, the Lord gave me strength and a sense of peace which I still feel to this day. Please know that I still struggle with pride and placing Christ first in every aspect of my life, and I have challenges like everyone else. But knowing that He will forgive me, love me, guide me, and bless me keeps me coming back again and again to the place where I pray the words, "I surrender Lord. Please lead me."

ARE THERE PRACTICAL STEPS WE CAN TAKE?

The choice to surrender to Christ and place Him first takes commitment, and the journey to get there is difficult. I know a lot of good, smart Catholic men who have been deeply moved by an emotional meeting, weekend, inspirational book, or personal tragedy to make this commitment, only to lapse back into "me-first" behavior weeks later. It can happen to anyone. This commitment has to be firm and will require sincerity, diligence, and sacrifice.

Here are some practical actions I have learned from some great Catholic men on how to help put Christ and His will first in my life.

START AND END YOUR DAY WITH PRAYER

Speak to Christ through prayer and ask Him to lead you. Pray that His will be done and offer up everything to Him. Consider this prayer: "Lord, please make me a channel for your will. Help me be humble, selfless, and able to discern your plan for my life. I love you and thank you for every blessing. I ask you to lead me and guide my actions today and every day."

FOLLOW MARY'S EXAMPLE

Our Blessed Mother is the greatest example of trusting God and her yes should inspire us to do the same. Say a daily Rosary to invoke her help, or, if a full Rosary seems like a bit much, start with five decades or even one decade—*any* Marian prayer is better than *no* Marian prayer. "From Mary we learn to surrender to God's Will in all things. From Mary we learn to trust even when all hope seems gone. From Mary we learn to love Christ her Son and the Son of God!" (St. Pope John Paul II, Homily of October 6, 1979).

EDUCATE YOURSELF

Study the faith. Read the Bible and the Catechism of the Catholic Church, or a short meditation each day. I highly recommend *The Way* and/or *The Furrow* by St. Josemaría

Escrivá (*The Way, The Furrow, The Forge* is a full single volume edition), *Jesus Shock* by Peter Kreeft, *Jesus of Nazareth* by Pope Emeritus Benedict XVI, *Introduction to the Devout Life* by St. Francis de Sales, and *The Imitation of Christ* by Thomas A. Kempis.

BECOME PASSIONATE ABOUT THE EUCHARIST

Do you want to fully experience Christ and be closer to Him? Seek out the True Presence of Christ in the Eucharist in daily Mass when possible, and spend quiet time before the Blessed Sacrament in Eucharistic Adoration every week. "When you have received Him, stir up your heart to do Him homage; speak to Him about your spiritual life, gazing upon Him in your soul where He is present for your happiness; welcome Him as warmly as possible, and behave outwardly in such a way that your actions may give proof to all of His Presence" (St. Francis de Sales). See more on this in chapter five.

PURSUE JOY, NOT HAPPINESS

A former director of vocations for the Archdiocese of Atlanta gave a wonderful talk to the St. Peter Chanel Business Association some years ago in which he described the pursuit of happiness as the pursuit of the things of this world. We think we are seeking happiness in the bigger house, nicer car, better job, bigger paycheck, but do these things really bring happiness? His point was that all happiness must be preceded by *joy* and that all joy is *Christ-inspired*! My brothers, seek out and surrender your heart to Christ to find joy, and you will also find happiness.

You may be doing all of these things and much more, and I say thank you for showing us the way by your example. This is certainly not the definitive list, but these actions keep me focused on Christ's will and help me find my way back to Him when I get lost. As you consider the contents of this chapter and how it speaks to you, please be mindful that you can't simply "add Jesus to your life" and share control with Him. He requires all of us, all of the time. In return for our trustful surrender, He will fill us with His strength, His love, His peace, and shape us into the fathers, husbands, friends, leaders and Catholics we always wanted to be. With His strength within us, we will find ourselves often giving to others and sharing our newfound selfless love to the people in our lives. In the end, ask yourself, "What do I really lose by surrendering to Christ?" Then, ask yourself, "What do I lose by *failing* to surrender to Christ?"

Over the last few years I have gotten to know a remarkable Catholic husband, leader, and evangelist for our faith, Dr. Bill Thierfelder. He is president of Belmont Abbey College, a Catholic liberal arts college near Charlotte, North Carolina and the author of *Less Than A Minute To Go: The Secret to World-Class Performance in Sport, Business and Everyday Life.*

Prior to his appointment as president of Belmont Abbey College, Dr. Thierfelder was president of the legendary fitness company York Barbell. He has delivered hundreds of presentations on topics related to faith, sports, education, medicine, and business, as well as testifying before the United States Congress in matters related to religious liberty. He is a Knight of Malta and lives just outside of Charlotte with his wife Mary and their ten children.

Despite this impressive list of accomplishments, Dr. Thierfelder is one of the humblest men I know. It comes across clearly in his talks, his writing, his work for the Church, and even the way he greets students as he walks across the beautiful campus at Belmont Abbey College.

Dr. Thierfelder, I was very interested in capturing your thoughts and perspectives on the challenges Catholic men (and all men for that matter!) have with pride. Why is pride a major obstacle in living our Catholic faith?

> "Pride is the beginning of all sin. This inordinate self-love is the foundation upon which every obstacle in a man's life is built.
>
> "Men typically have a natural ability and endurance to focus on a single task until it is accomplished, even to the detriment of everyone around them. There is a competitiveness within men that makes every task a matter of winning or losing. This intense drive to 'win' can often become a selfish and self-centered occupation. Our society further reinforces that drive by promoting the 'winners' and cutting the 'losers.' This can lead to the justification of a win at all costs mentality that will ultimately hurt them and everyone they love. What is the point to winning a contest if you lose the most important things in your life? (cf. Mark 8:36)"

From your own personal experiences and observations, do Catholic men of any age recognize when pride is interfering in their marriages, relationships with their children, careers, and the practice of their Catholic faith? Why do we struggle to see it and what can we do to be more aware of the presence of pride?

"The insidiousness of pride is that it leads us to say, 'You are the problem, not me.' Our need to be 'right' or 'good enough' in order to get the love we desire, often prevents us from seeing the truth which is, 'I am the problem' or 'I don't know.' Because men are expected to be leaders and to have all the answers, they can come to think and believe that they know what is best in any given situation. After all, how often have you met a man that likes to ask for directions when he is lost?

"Overcoming vice requires awareness. If you don't know what you did there is no way to change or improve it. The same is true for overcoming your pride. Ask yourself, 'How well do I listen to others? Am I preparing my answer before I have listened to all they had to say?' A good rule of thumb when speaking with someone is to first consider before you respond, 'Is it true? Does it need to be said? Will it make a difference?' If you can say, 'Yes' to all three it is probably worth saying. If not, keep listening! This will help you to focus on others and not yourself."

You have mentioned prayer, humility, and surrender as the antidotes to pride and I wholeheartedly agree. If we can acknowledge the presence of sinful pride in our lives, how do we embrace humility and surrender when these actions are so difficult for most men?

"Humility is recognizing, 'I am nothing, I know nothing, and I have nothing.' This is not low self-esteem or a false humility because, after all, if you are standing next to God what are you bragging about? There is a wonderful freedom that comes with that realization. I don't have to be something I am not. I am called to be exactly what God wants me to be and to give my all in everything I do. You can never 'lose' or be 'put down' because you correctly see that you are already in the dust. This frees you up to actually perform at your best. You can now put all of your attention and talent on the task at hand which usually results in your best performance. And you are not doing it because people will clap you on the back and tell you that you are great, but rather because you want to give God all that you have.

"Humility is taking on great things without fear because you know the source of greatness is God and not you. For this reason humble people can do great things!"

As you reflect on your own life, can you recall a specific instance where you have been derailed by the sin of pride and what happened to help you get back on track?

"Early in my career it would bother me when I read about how other professionals in my field had succeeded in some way. I tended to criticize their accomplishments and find reasons why they were not deserving of it. Although I was not conscious of it at the time, I was doing it in an attempt to prove that I was the 'best' and deserving of all the honors. I never said, 'I am the best,' but by putting others down I was in fact saying it.

> "You might be tempted to think, 'But what if you and I are the best at what we do?' Well that would be wonderful but why would we feel it necessary to put others down? Why couldn't we be happy for their success? The very fact that we are so concerned that others might somehow get credit or be acknowledged for some accomplishment reveals our pride. Like Lucifer, the prince of pride, not even God can be the best.
>
> "Reading the writings of the saints was particularly helpful in overcoming this fatal flaw. *Trustful Surrender to Divine Providence: The Secret to Peace and Happiness, Abandonment to Divine Providence,* and *The Devout Life* just to name a few, helped me to see the truth of my place in the world. I came to clearly understand and believe that anything I possessed was in fact a gift from God. I was one of the servants in Matthew 25:14–30. I was given according to my ability everything; physically, mentally, and spiritually—and so was everyone else! They were called to be good stewards, just like me, and to double what they had been given.
>
> "This freed me up to do the best that I could with all that I had been blessed with and to be happy when others did the same thing."

If you could distill the volumes of Catholic teaching about the sin of pride into an actionable "accountability plan" for Catholic men, what would this practical plan look like?

"I would suggest keeping it simple. First, God is King and I am not! All that I have is His. I am called to double the talents He has given me, to give back 100 percent. That means everything I have is a gift.

"Take a minute or two and write down on a piece of paper all of the things in your life that are invaluable, meaning beyond worth. You wouldn't trade them for all the money in the world. After about a minute most people have stopped writing. Let's review your list. For example did you write down your brain stem? Or how about your left and right retinas? Or each of the nuclei contained in every cell of your body? Initially you probably had a look on your face that said, 'What is he talking about?' But think about it. Can you live with cells that have no nucleus? No. Now reconsider your list. You probably wrote down big things like, my health, my family, and so on, without considering all of the invaluable things that make up each one. To make a proper list you would need an almost infinite number of pads and pencils to write down all of the things that could not be bought with all of the world's treasure.

"We are wealthy beyond understanding. If we had everything taken away from us today and we lived another hundred years, we could never sufficiently thank God for all that He has given us to this point in time. In the face of such immense generosity how can we not help being humbled to the ground?

"Having profound gratitude and humility will increase your desire to do God's will in all things rather than your own. The Blessed Mother tells you how to do it with five of the most powerful words ever written, *Do whatever he tells you* (John 2:5). Your obedience to her words ensures your protection against the sin of pride.

"This does not require some major undertaking on your part. St. Thérèse the Little Flower was known for the 'little way.' She made it a practice of doing the smallest things with love and humility. Think about each day. What 'little' things can you do to remind yourself of your proper place in God's plan?

"Here are just a few suggestions that might help you overcome pride and acquire the virtue of humility. Start with the one, or part of one, that is easiest for you to do. Add another one as you can, asking the Holy Spirit to guide you.

"If possible, find a good spiritual director; go to confession often, at the very least once a month; receive the Eucharist weekly, daily when possible; see Christ in and be Christ to everyone you meet, especially those who annoy you because they need your love the most; listen before speaking; when you are wrong admit it, apologize, do reparation and move on. Instead of saying, 'I am proud of you,' say, 'You bring me great joy.' Be obedient according to your station in life. Train yourself to instantly say, 'Thank you, Jesus' when things go well and, especially, when things go bad (see 1 Thess 5:18). Read some Scripture

> or writings of the saints every day, even if it is just a sentence or two. Surround yourself with things that remind you about God. Keep sacramentals in the car, at work, and on your person. Pray the Rosary or five decades of it every evening with your family even if it means calling in on the speaker phone, and never forget that this life passes in a billionth of a second (see Pope St. Pius X's Prayer to St. Joseph the Worker)."

So what does this chapter on pride and surrender reveal to us? It reminds us that praying for humility every day is necessary. It reminds us that surrender and conversion is ongoing, not a one-time event. It makes us appreciate even more those candid friends who are unafraid to speak truth into our lives. It should make us grateful for the Sacrament of Reconciliation where we can confess our sins and be made whole. I hope it makes us grateful for a forgiving God who loves us.

QUESTIONS FOR REFLECTION

1. Before reading this chapter, did I make the connection between surrender and pride? Do I now more fully understand that I must give up control? That Christ wants all of me, not just the portion I am prepared to share?
2. If I am honest, how many of the obstacles to surrender shared by the author do I relate to in my own experience? Are any others getting in the way?
3. Dr. Thierfelder offered prayer, humility, and surrender as the antidotes to pride. Part of

accepting these antidotes is the need to practice self-awareness. Am I self-aware? Do I realize when my pride gets in the way?

4. Dr. Thierfelder offered a simple action plan to combat pride in the last paragraph of his interview. Am I doing any of these actions now? Will I commit to begin and who will hold me accountable?

CHAPTER THREE

Let It Go

Unhealthy attachments to things and people of this world
do not free us to seek the health of our soul but rather
distract us from the true needs we have:
peace, contentment, gratitude, joy.
These are what the soul long for and
can only be found truly in God.
— Fr. Martin Connor —

I grew up in a home where both my parents worked to make ends meet. There were years that my dad worked two jobs to help support our family. We had few extras, but we had what we needed. If I wanted spending money I worked a number of jobs to earn it. What our family did have in abundance was love, encouragement, and a focus on the importance of values. My parents always made time for my sister and me, and family dinner time was sacred. They were genuinely interested in what we were doing at school. As tired as my father was after work, he would play catch with me every evening and on weekends. My mother was our emotional bedrock and I always admired what a great team she and my father formed. We had rules in our house and I knew the boundaries that I could not cross. Faith was very important to my parents and church and prayer were staples in our household. My childhood was by no means perfect, but I am grateful for my experience and how it has shaped me today.

I suspect that many of us have similar fond memories and "Norman Rockwell moments" in our past. I would suggest that a bond that connects most of our various childhood experiences is simplicity. We didn't have as many distractions. Technology was still under our control (versus the pervasive influence it has on us today) and values and character still mattered. You probably found fewer obstacles back then to your relationship with Christ. I am a realist in my forties and understand very well the technology-driven world in which we live, but as I grow older I am hardening against a neo-modernist "everything goes" version of the future and looking more to the lessons of the past for guidance.

I am increasingly alarmed by the obsession and addiction to consumerism and materialism that seems to drive so many families today. The media and retail advertisers have insinuated themselves into every electronic device or print product we own, use, and see every day. We have been sold for decades on the idea of a lifestyle that is filled with fun, convenience and, dare I say, guilt, if we don't pursue this artificial paradise. The push is to buy, buy, buy, and then buy some more!

The focus on acquiring material goods drives many of us to work harder and harder to make more money to buy bigger houses, nicer cars, and cooler gadgets. This obsession often pulls both parents into the work force to support their lifestyle, keep up with the neighbors, or satisfy some deep inner emptiness. There is nothing wrong with a nice lifestyle, but how much is enough? And more importantly, can we take it with us at the end of our lives?

In Matthew 6:19–21 our Lord said, *Do not lay up for yourselves treasures on earth, where moth and rust consume and where thieves break in and steal. But store up treasures in heaven, where neither moth nor decay destroys, nor thieves break in and steal. . . . For where your treasure is, there will your heart be also.* This clear direction from Jesus means we need to take better inventory of our lives. We need to make sure that God is not just one of our priorities, but instead He must be the top priority. Jesus again addressed this subject in Matthew 6:24, 33–34: *No one can serve two masters; for either he will hate the one and love the other, or he will be devoted to the one and despise the other. You cannot serve God and mammon . . . . But seek first his kingdom (of God) and his righteousness, and all these things shall be yours as well. Do not be anxious about tomorrow; tomorrow will be anxious for itself. Let the day's own trouble be sufficient for the day.*

This focus on acquiring the things of this world takes our focus away from God. Again, please don't misunderstand me. Supporting our family comfortably is not in itself wrong. I am talking about the *excessive* pursuit of material goods that takes our focus away from Him. There is a word that squarely addresses this problem: *detachment.* As Francis Fernandez wrote in his excellent book series, *In Conversation with God*: "Effective detachment from things demands sacrifice. Any detachment which is not hard is not real. Christian life is such that it calls for a radical change in attitude towards earthly goods. We must acquire them and use them not as an end to themselves, but as a means of serving God, the family and society. The objective of a Christian is not to accumulate more and more but to love Christ more and more through his work and his family as well as through material goods" (Vol. 3, 109–110).

Think about the key words we place before the material things we desire during the course of a day: "I want," "I need," or "I love." Now, replace these material things with Christ and use the same key words. We should all *want, need,* and *love* Christ, and our thoughts should always be of Him.

Seeking more insight into the need for "detachment," I reached out to a well-respected priest who is actively involved with Catholic men's ministries. Father Martin Connor, LC is a Baltimore native and one of eight children, the last two of which are Legionary priests. He entered the Legionaries of Christ in 1990 after graduating from Boston College with degrees in philosophy and theology. He also holds a graduate degree in philosophy from the Pontifical *Atheneum Regina Apostolorum* in Rome. He has taught extensively on St. Pope John Paul II's theology of the body and is at present part of the national clergy board for the Theology of the Body Institute in Philadelphia. Currently he resides in Atlanta and is chaplain to both the men of the Regnum Christi and the local chapter of the Lumen Institute.

Father, through the observations you have made during your priesthood and work as chaplain of the Atlanta Fatherhood Forum, what are the biggest obstacles between Catholic men and Christ?

"I would say that the two biggest obstacles today for men are the problem of lust and of materialism. Both have in fact the same root problem: independence from God rooted in a spirit of idolatry. We tend to idolize the created world rather than worship the one true God. Is there any wonder why God warned us in the first commandment about idolatry: 'You shall have no other gods before me'? It was like He was saying, Guys, if you can get this right then the rest will flow. You need me and don't try to go it alone. We men in particular do not like to 'feel' our neediness. Just ask the women in our lives. We hate feeling dependent on others or the least bit inadequate. Many times we just wear a mask of confidence but inside we are frightened of failing, of not measuring up. Just take, for example, when a man loses his job. Many times this experience can take the form of literally an existential tragedy, striking a man at his very depths, making him question his very self-worth. I believe the reason for this is that it nails the very heart of the problem, his independence. Joblessness makes a man very dependent. With the downturn in our economy I have witnessed firsthand how such difficult experiences bring men back to a strong faith life rooted in a loving dependence on God's plan.

"The problem of lust is a problem of losing balance. God told Adam to go and be master of His creation (Gen 1: 28–29). When sin entered the world it created an imbalance in man's heart. Hence with lust man seeks dominance and control over another rather than respect and esteem. We are wired with these very strong impulses towards physical beauty. These passions can drive us to seek disordered fulfillment in all kinds of ways rather than controlling and channeling them towards the right way of being. Why shouldn't I act on them since this is how I am made, right? Yet God has created the human person with a special dignity that is more than mere animal. We are thinking and choosing creatures, rational animals, who with our freedom can choose what we become with our decisions. We can become less than we are, than we were created to be. The porn addict is a perfect example: jaded, broken, and totally turned inward, incapable of interpersonal relationship, especially with women. Is he really a better man for acting on his impulses?

"Greed or materialism is also a problem of wanting to be in control. If I can just have enough 'financial security' then all will be well. Wealth is false security. It is just another lie from the evil one that we cannot make work without God."

You mentioned "attachment" and the need to let go of things which don't matter. Can you expand on that subject?

"We come into this world like sponges. Just watch children grow up. They absorb everything—the good and the bad of their parents and their surroundings. Yet this is how God made us so that we 'learn the ropes,' mature, and get on in life. However, because we are so inclined to 'assimilate' what is around us we can also begin to make such things and people the end all, be all. In other words, we can start expecting such things to be our happiness, to fulfill us. They become attachments. There is no creature—material or immaterial—that can ultimately fulfill the human heart. Only our Lord and Creator can do this. So when I talk about attachments, I am referring to our tendency as human beings to place our time, attention, and energy on what is temporal rather than what is eternal, never changing. We all agree that physical health is important and the time and money we might dedicate to this reality is significant. However, given that we are more than just physical organisms—*body and soul*—we need to look after the spirit. "What is the state of my soul? How am I feeding it? Unhealthy attachments to things and people of this world do not free us to seek the health of our soul, but rather distract us from the true needs we have: peace, contentment, gratitude, joy. These are what the soul long for and can only be found truly in God."

In our modern materialistic culture where men are bombarded with messages about false idols and encouraged to acquire things they don't need, how would you counsel us to fight back?

"We become materialistic easily because we do not think clearly. Time for God is absolutely crucial. Prayer gives us the ability to think clearly. It gives us a compass of what is right and wrong, and points us in the direction of heavenly realities which are the never-changing truths that should govern our lives. Remember we are pilgrims in this life. We should not be *too* comfortable with what this life offers. We were not made for this world so why place all our hopes here? Therefore, the first lesson is to make sure that your spiritual life is strong, that you are praying so you can keep your head and heart clear to make the right decisions, discover the false idols in your life, reject them, and follow what is truly important. The desires of your heart will lead to what is infinite, never ending, and only God is infinite.

"Second, it is crucial that you get a handle on what keeps you from a God centered life and you start putting boundaries on those things. For most it begins with your financial world. This is not a conversation people like to have but it is absolutely essential. We must tithe intentionally! It is much more important to have clear what you are giving to God every month, quarter, and year, than what you are going to do for Christmas with the family, when you are going on your next vacation, or what school your kids will go to. These questions may be important but they will not have a strong hold over your heart like your financial world does and thus direct your behavior. When it comes to their finances, most people think they are pretty generous but very few know the actual hard number of their generous 'tithing' to others needs. Numbers do not lie. Hence why I challenge people to put order in their finances and find that monthly and annual tithing number they are giving. You would be surprised that when someone takes me up on the challenge what they often find is the hard number is quite a bit less than they guessed.

"Why is tithing, or better, the ordering of your finances so important? What we believe as Christians is that we are saved. Saved from what? From ourselves. Our whole world is (economically or otherwise) driven to please 'self.' We are professionals at pleasing ourselves. Yet our faith is about being 'selfless' like Christ. If your first intention is to give your 'first fruits to God' (like He in fact asks in Exodus 23:19), then you will get all your other priorities straight. You will set a tone for your life that is 'other-centered.' If you blow this one, it is inevitable, given our fallen nature, that you will become quite selfish and most likely begin to fail in the other key areas of your life, like marriage and parenting which already demand so much!"

Do these disordered attachments affect our generosity towards the Church, serving others, and charity in general? How?

"Without any question disordered attachments affect our generosity. They are just that—disordered; in other words, not 'ordered rightly' towards the right ends. Our end game is heaven, and to aspire to that total attachment to what God wants for us demands 'detachment' from what we *think* we need. In doing so, we find that our previous 'needs' were really selfish 'wants.' In other words, what we want is many times not what we need. And it is not like God does not know what will give us utter bliss, total fulfillment, and the thrill of joy. His plans are much better than our plans. God knows our hearts and is tirelessly dedicated to bringing us to Him, to filling our hearts with what is the true food of happiness. A strong spiritual life keeps us from false needs that breed uncontrollable wants. The key manifestation of a strong spiritual life is an 'other-centered life': service to your family and your community rather than just thinking about yourself and your needs. This is why the baptized are called not just to seek holiness but to build the kingdom of Christ. In other words, when we do apostolate, when we are the hands and feet of Christ to others, there is detachment from self that comes from this. When you opt not to get involved in serving others, you opt out of the essence of what makes you a follower of Christ in the first place."

How can a Catholic man begin to develop a mindset of generosity and let go of these attachments in today's world? What are practical actions we can take to make this a reality?

"Generosity is not simply 'cutting a check.' We men need to act. We need to execute on things that hold first place in our life. If we do not, then we call that 'lip service,' and there is not a *real* man out there who likes just 'lip service.' Jesus Christ does not like it either. 'Not everyone who says to me, 'Lord, Lord,' will enter the kingdom of heaven, but he who does the will of my Father who is in heaven' (Matthew 7:21).

"What keeps a man generous and selfless is what *calls him to come out of himself*, what is most important to him. First his wife and family or those he loves. As a daily self-examination I need to ask, What am I doing for people in my life on a day to day basis that goes beyond the 'providing' component, albeit very important part of my life? Who am I giving myself to? We men must be able to answer that with concrete examples on a *daily basis* in order for us to combat our naturally self-serving tendencies that are so strong in us. Some acceptable answers to these questions are:

- I make breakfast for my wife and children in the morning before school (not just once a month).
- I sacrifice sleep to pray in the morning (not just once a week).
- Pots and pans are my duty after dinner.
- My wife's body is holy and deserves my reverence and respect.
- Spiritual leadership in the family translates into 'I initiate prayer,' not my wife.
- Carpooling for sports is a shared responsibility between my wife and me.

"A daily examen at the end of your day will keep your ego-centered tendencies in check and with the help of God's grace make you a more loving and dedicated man.

"This follows the age old wisdom of Socrates: 'An unexamined life is not worth living.'"

One man who left behind what the world holds most dear in order to fully serve God and the Church is Tom Peterson, president and founder of Catholics Come Home. Following twenty-five years as an award-winning advertising executive, Tom Peterson's life would radically change forever after receiving a transforming spiritual conversion while on a Catholic men's retreat. Soon afterward he founded VirtueMedia (pro-life) and CatholicsComeHome.org. In the first six years, Catholics Come Home has aired Catholic evangelization commercials in thirty-six dioceses and nationally, helping lead nearly five hundred thousand souls home to the Catholic Church. Tom is passionate about our Catholic faith and devoted to his wife, three daughters, and first grandson.

Tom, I have long appreciated the story of your faith journey and the reconversion to the Catholic Church you experienced many years ago. One aspect of your story that has always intrigued me was your decision to downsize and simplify your life and shed what you described as your "idols." Can you elaborate?

> "Absolutely! When many of us think of the word idol, we may think of a statue of a pagan god. That's accurate, but idols also take the form of career, money, beauty, a large home, a nice car, exotic vacations, or even the admiration of our friends and peers. The Church teaches that even if one of these things takes primacy in our lives, then we are worshipping an idol.
>
> "This observation comes from my own experience as well because there was a period in my life which was filled with idols. God was relegated to a small corner of my heart as I pursued a lifestyle and lived a life devoid of the things which truly matter. It took time, but I began to realize that these worldly idols had to vanish for God to be first in my life. That decision and the painful process that followed has made all the difference for me and my family, and I am truly

blessed to have been given a second chance and to have experienced God's love and mercy."

Do you see our Catholic men of today experiencing the same issues with idols and the right priorities?

"I do, and it is getting worse. I think we need to start by recognizing that God wants us to be happy, truly happy. He is our loving heavenly Father and He made us for a great purpose. He wants to reveal His love to us and have that love with everyone we encounter. But there are obstacles that keep us from doing this. We are working harder and longer to buy things which do not make us happy. We are often trying to maintain a lifestyle that requires both husband and wife to work full time, instead of more modest lifestyle which allows for a happy and well-adjusted family focused on loving and serving God.

"This is not only about lifestyle, but also about how we are living. Society is demanding more and more from our young people and the competition factor can be overwhelming for our kids. Many families I know are racing from sporting event to recitals to various other activities without making time to just be together. We have forgotten how to relax and hang out in each other's company. Families need to pray together and go to Mass together and do Eucharistic Adoration together. They can and should serve the least of our brothers and sisters in the community. So, chasing idols and the wrong priorities are hurting so many families today, and Catholic men must rise to the challenge of saying no when appropriate and being leaders in their homes."

Tom, I know your walk back to a fully active practice of your Catholic faith and your roles as founder of Catholics Come Home and Virtue Media were greatly aided by prayer and the Sacrament of Reconciliation. Can you share how these catalysts helped you?

"Without prayer we cease to communicate with God. We simply can't know His will without an active prayer life throughout every day. Reconciliation is the most underutilized sacrament in the Church, yet provides us with sacramental graces and forgiveness to start fresh and begin anew. God is merciful and wants to shower us with His love, yet we need to accept His gift. If you haven't been to Confession in the last two months, make the commitment to go this week. It changed my life and countless others and will bless you and your family too."

Tom, one last question. When you think about how much of your energy and time was devoted to supporting a materialistic worldly lifestyle years ago versus the way you spend your energy and time today, can you describe in simple terms the difference in your life, your family's life, and the lives of those you encounter each day?

"When we take the focus off ourselves and focus on God's will for our life, we begin to experience the adventure of the new evangelization—God's true plan and purpose for each of our lives. Nothing will make us happier or more fulfilled than doing and living

God's perfect will. He customizes this for each of us. With a sincere heart, ask the Holy Spirit to guide your path, live the Commandments, pray and help others, and watch the miracles begin!"

QUESTIONS FOR REFLECTION

1. As I ponder the lessons of this chapter, do I recognize any disordered attachments in my life? What are they?
2. Have I fallen into the trap of trying to serve two masters? Do I recognize that this is really not possible?
3. As I consider my real priorities in light of what the author, Fr. Connor, and Tom Peterson have shared, how would I rank what is important to me today? Prior to reading this chapter, were my actions aligning with supporting this list of what is important?
4. What will I do differently, starting today, to shed myself of the things in life that do not matter? Who will hold me accountable?

CHAPTER FOUR

Being a Man of Prayer

Many of the spiritually indifferent Catholic men
I have encountered are struggling in their prayer lives,
and yet turning our thoughts to Him in prayer,
thanking Him, and asking for His help can be so easy
if we will only surrender and acknowledge
that we can't do it alone.
— Author —

As I was writing this chapter I reflected on my experiences as a Catholic from my conversion in 2005 until now. One of the biggest obstacles for me in the early days of my faith journey was the lack of a prayer life. I knew I needed to pray, but I couldn't ever remember sincerely praying about anything. I was struggling with the typical male challenge of asking for help, especially asking God for help! I rationalized this by thinking, "Who am I to bother Him with my petty problems?"

I went to one of our parish deacons, shared my prayer challenges with him and asked for guidance. He looked at me with a smile and said I was approaching prayer in the wrong way. "Don't worry about asking for help just yet," he said. His counsel was to simply go to the Lord with thanks and be grateful for the blessings in my life. The light bulb went on and I finally got it. Eventually, I learned to ask God for help and guidance, but my prayer life really began when I learned to simply offer thanks to God for the blessings in my life. There have been bumps along the way and dry spells, but my prayer life has continued to unfold and grow with each passing day.

Let's be honest. Praying can be difficult. Men, I don't pretend to be an expert on prayer, but I know my life has been made exponentially better because I *do* pray. I have experienced countless challenges as a husband, father, and businessman that I could not have overcome without prayer. I would like to share with you the steps in my prayer journey as a Catholic man, lessons I have learned and insights into how I pray in the hope you will find my experiences to be helpful.

Step One of my prayer life was *learning to thank God and be grateful.* As I learned from that helpful deacon many years ago, going to Him in prayer and reflecting on the blessings in my life every day is how I learned to appreciate and acknowledge God's role in my life. To this day, I do not begin a prayer without thanking Him.

Step Two was learning *to ask for forgiveness.* I go to the Sacrament of Reconciliation frequently, but it is still important for me to ask the Lord for His pardon and forgiveness when I commit a sin, which is more frequent than I care to admit. It has become a daily examination of conscience for me to reflect on where I have failed Him, and ask for forgiveness and the grace to avoid committing that sin again.

STEP THREE was *asking for His help and guidance.* This is also when I learned to pray for others and their intentions. I think men in general struggle with asking for help and I am certainly no exception. My growing prayer life and deepening faith has given me the humility to realize that I don't have all the answers and that Jesus absolutely wants to help me. In the early days, I would tentatively ask for help with the *big* stuff like getting my family into heaven, blessing our priests and deacons, healing a sick friend, and so on. Now, I am very comfortable asking for His help and guidance in every facet of my life.

STEP FOUR was *learning to completely unburden myself to the Lord.* This has occurred only in the last few years. I am inclined to carry my stress, frustrations, worries, and fears like a hidden weight around my neck. As I got better at going to the Lord for help, I began asking Him to lighten these mental and emotional burdens. I am so grateful that I now can go to Him and give Him my work stress, concerns about my children's future, or anything else that is weighing me down. *Come to me, all who labor and are heavy laden, and I will give you rest. Take my yoke upon you, and learn from me; for I am gentle and lowly in heart, and you will find rest for your souls. For my yoke is easy, and my burden is light* (Matthew 11:28–29).

STEP FIVE has been a somewhat recent change as I *have learned to pray for acceptance.* A few years ago one of our parish priests challenged me and my wife not only to pray for the healing and independent future we desire for our older son who has autism, but to pray for acceptance as well. By only asking for healing, he said we were essentially asking God to take back His creation and make him better. This was a profound realization for us and it has spilled over into other areas of my life. I now pray for acceptance of the challenges and difficult moments in my life and ask to learn from them rather than asking God to "fix" them. This new approach has positively affected every aspect of my life and I am grateful.

Step Six has been *my increasing prayers for the intercession of our Blessed Mother and the saints.* Seeking the intercession of Mary when I pray my Rosary, or in moments when I desperately need her strength has been an incredible blessing. When I face challenges as a husband or father, I go to St. Joseph and seek his help as the incredible example he should be for all men. St. Michael the Archangel, St. Philomena, and St. Thomas More are also among the saints whose help I frequently seek.

I am hopeful there will be more evolving steps in prayer growth for me if I am humble and committed to deepening my relationship with Christ. St. Teresa of Avila, a doctor of the Church, wrote on the stages of prayer in her book *The Interior Castle.* I sincerely hope to reach the contemplative and mystical prayer life she describes in her works and pray that Christ will lead me there.

These are some important lessons I have learned (and keep learning!) in my prayer life and would like to share.

JUST DO IT!

If we don't schedule prayer time and stick to it, it will not happen. Put your prayer life on your calendar. Ask yourself if you would be willing to spend only thirty minutes a day with your loved ones. Hopefully the answer is a resounding *no!* Ok, then why do we struggle to give the Lord at least thirty minutes a day in prayer? How we pray is not nearly as important as the act of praying itself.

PREPARE OUR HEARTS AND MINDS FOR PRAYER

We must have the right attitudes of humility and faith that God can and will help us before we start praying. Reading Scripture, the Magnificat, or a book of meditations such as *The Way, Furrow, The Forge* (single volume edition) by St. Josemaría Escrivá every day before prayer will help prepare our heads and hearts to approach Christ in a more intentional and meaningful way.

OVERCOMING THE "DRY PATCHES"

We all experience dryness in our prayers or have trouble focusing. We may feel that God is not listening. We may fall into the trap of asking God to validate what we want instead of submitting to His will. I am certain that most of us will experience this, but keep at it! Mother Teresa's book revealed decades of dryness and despair in her prayer life and yet she persevered.

DON'T ALLOW WORK AND OUR BUSYNESS TO BE AN EXCUSE

If we are serious about improving our prayer lives, we will stop making prayer conform to our day and make our day conform to our prayer lives. If we deem it important, it will happen. Also, consider integrating prayer into a workout while running or during your commute to and from work. If you seriously feel as though you don't have a free minute in your day and that adding prayer would be unduly burdensome, I suggest sitting down and taking an objective inventory of your day to see how and where you are spending your time. The results may be shocking. "Everyone needs thirty minutes of personal prayer time each day, unless they are too busy to pray—in which case, they need an hour!" (St. Francis de Sales).

PRAY MORE, LISTEN MORE

I want to listen more in prayer and not ramble on about what I need. I want to let Him speak to me and I need to be still and ready to listen. I need to avoid asking God to validate decisions I have already made. As I learned a few years ago, prayer is every time you turn your thoughts to God and away from yourself.

WITHOUT PRAYER, OUR FAITH WILL DIE

We simply will not grow our relationship with Christ unless we do so through prayer. According to the Catechism (2744): "Prayer is a vital necessity. Proof from the contrary is no less convincing: if we do not allow the Spirit to lead us, we fall back into the slavery of sin [cf. Gal 5:16–25]."

Finally, I would like to share some insights into exactly *how* I pray in the hope that this might offer practical ideas for your own prayer lives:

WHEN I AM IN A QUIET PLACE...

Upon waking in the morning before the rest of my family I say a brief prayer of thanks to start the day. After coffee and a little spiritual reading I pray about what I have read and about the challenges facing me that day or the special intentions of a friend or loved one. My family prays together every night and we are trying to introduce a family Rosary. I have also been a Eucharistic Adoration Guardian for over seven years. This is the best hour of my week as I pray before the True Presence of Christ in the Blessed Sacrament. I pray in Mass to be worthy to receive the gift of the Eucharist, and I pray a prayer of thanksgiving for this wonderful gift after I receive communion.

WHEN I AM ENGAGED IN MY WORK DAY . . .

I try to go to daily Mass at my parish or another parish near my office when I can, but I hope to do a better job of this in the future as my day is always better after receiving Communion. An important part of my daily prayer is the daily examen, developed by the Jesuits. I place this on my iPhone calendar and am reminded five times a day to stop for a few minutes and reflect on the events and people around me and then pray. Each stopping point has a specific purpose and you can learn more about this helpful prayer exercise in appendix three. Also, I pray a blessing over my meal and invite my companions to join me.

WHEN I AM ON THE GO . . .

I have found replacing radio time with prayer time to and from work has been a huge help to my sanity! I often pray the Morning Offering and the Angelus when I am in my car. This may seem strange, but I prefer to pray my Rosary when I am running the trails near my home or on the treadmill. I love the idea of integrating an important prayer with an important activity. Those on the go may also find Masstimes.org and smartphone app to be very helpful in finding the nearest churches for Mass and visits to the Blessed Sacrament.

FOOD FOR THOUGHT . . .

Praying more can seem overwhelming if you are busy like me, but if you add up all the praying I just shared, it is well over an hour a day. It helps me to break it down this way, and I can't stress enough the importance of putting your prayer life on your calendar. As I said before, if it is not scheduled it will not happen. Also, don't let my encouragement of a prayer routine ever discourage you from spontaneous prayer as situations warrant it.

Brothers, I certainly don't have all the answers and I am no expert on prayer. I simply want to share with you as someone who struggles with similar challenges as you that my prayer life and my faith journey have grown together. I didn't have any kind of prayer life before 2005 and now I couldn't imagine living a life without one. To me, prayer is anytime that I turn my attention to God and away from myself. It can be accomplished in a variety of ways and acts. Remember that feeling worthy or inspired is *not* a great barometer for measuring the value of our prayer life. Praying for the *desire for prayer* is worthwhile and a good start.

What if we desire to explore an even richer and deeper prayer life? For advice in this area, I reached out to Dan Burke, a man many in the Catholic world know for his blogging, speaking, and 2012 award-winning book, *Navigating the Spiritual Life: Spiritual Direction and the Journey to God.* Dan is a passionate Catholic. Beyond his contagious love for Jesus and His Church, Dan is a grateful husband, father of four, and the founder of Catholic Spiritual Direction (www.RCSpiritualDirection.com)—the most widely read blog on the topic of authentic Catholic spirituality. Dan is the executive director of and writer for EWTN's *National Catholic Register* (www.NCRegister.com), a regular co-host on Register Radio, and an author and speaker who provides webinars. He travels to share his conversion story and the great riches that the Church provides us through authentic Catholic spirituality.

Dan has been featured on EWTN's Journey Home program (www.EWTN.com) and numerous radio programs.

Dan, in your travels around the country, what have you observed about the role of prayer in the lives of the Catholic men you have encountered?

> "If you are talking about men that I look up to, and men that are leading their families and making a difference in the Church and the world, and men that have great relationships with their wives and children, prayer plays a huge role in their lives. All of them take prayer very seriously and never end a day without significant time on their knees (both inside and outside of Mass)."

What appear to be the obstacles for men in pursuing more meaningful prayer lives?

> "Guys are wired to get stuff done. We are generally more task oriented and less relationally oriented, and prayer is a relational activity that naturally seems like a waste of time. Beyond that, there are a number of other forces that militate against a life of healthy prayer. Foremost is a secular religiosity that Pope Benedict called a 'practical atheism.' This is a form of Catholicism that is merely a social construct or a matter of heritage but not a matter of the heart.
>
> "Second to this empty religion is an absence of teaching about hell and the consequences of a life of practical atheism. Social research data shows that the majority of Catholics today live in almost complete

disregard for their faith outside of Mass, but then gladly come forward every Sunday to 'eat and drink damnation' rather than to encounter the living God who desires to meet them in the Eucharist. Beyond that is materialism that consumes excessive time at work and then indulgence in television, gaming, and other meaningless pursuits after work. So, we have weak and prayerless men, who by sin and sloth daily dilute their flaccid faith and predictably trod the path to hell, all the while, taking their spouses and children with them. All that said, I don't think focusing on external forces is the answer. Jesus was a man among men. He offered Himself to be sacrificed for those whom He loved and came to redeem. What man, if he is a real man, can meditate on this perfect act of self-giving and not be moved to live for something beyond himself? Men are called to be valiant warriors of virtue and faith, not effeminate followers who abdicate their responsibilities. There will be no excuses at the last judgment, and men who have been entrusted with the care of others but who have abdicated their responsibilities will likely hear, *I never knew you; depart from me, you evildoers* (Matthew 7:22)."

What has been the impact on your faith, your ministry, your family, and work resulting from your prayer life?

"This is a tough question. How would Mary answer the question, 'How did having the God of the universe as your son impact you?' Can we really measure these things? I suspect we can in the sense that to the degree that we draw closer to the Lord we grow in holiness and, given God's grace, in effectiveness in how we are able to serve others in apostolate and in other work. With respect to these factors I know that my wife would say that I have grown significantly in the past five years and we both attribute this progress to what I would call a life-changing relationship with Christ. As far as effectiveness in apostolate, the works I have been involved with in the past decade are marked by progress that I cannot attribute to mere human effort. The bottom line is that Christ is true to His word when He says, *[A]part from me you can do nothing*, and then again through St. Paul when he says, *I can do all things through Christ who strengthens me*."

What is your advice for a Catholic man with a desire to develop a richer prayer life? What are practical steps a prayer "novice" might pursue to get started?

"Start small and simple. Commit to a specific time and get an accountability partner. The importance of an accountability partner can't be overstated. The time commitment should be noted in your calendar weekly *before* you add anything else. Try to establish a specific place in your home that you use for prayer and nothing else. Let your family know about your new commitment and negotiate with them to help you keep the time and place sacred. Always pray when you are alert, and not tired. If you have no time, first, shrug off that foolish self-deception and then, in a manly march to victory, proceed immediately to your alarm clock and set it to wake you up a half-hour earlier. Then purchase a book entitled *The Better Part:*

> *A Christ-Centered Resource for Personal Prayer* and use it for your prayer time. This seems like a simple list but these basic steps will revolutionize your prayer life if you stick to them. Don't be a spineless sissy about this. Your soul depends upon it and so do those of your family."

If you were speaking to a group of Catholic men, from teenagers to senior citizens, what would you say to them about the vital necessity of prayer in our lives?

> "I would say that if having a relationship with Christ is necessary for us to be with Him in heaven for all eternity, then our very souls depend on it. St. Teresa of Avila says, 'He who neglects mental prayer needs no devil to carry him to hell. He brings himself there with his own hands.'"

Brothers, prayer is the key! If we are faithfully praying each day we are less likely to fall under the world's spell. It's not as difficult as we might think. Start the day with prayer. Before we check email or read the morning paper, offer the day and our burdens up to God, thank Him and ask for His forgiveness, help, and blessing. Integrate prayer into our daily commute and exercise time. Pray the Jesuit daily examen throughout the day. Pray for the courage to resist the temptations and distractions the world offers us each day. Be mindful that we should make our days conform to our prayer lives and not the other way around. Plan it and it will happen.

I always know how much better I feel after I pray. We can't remain apathetic about Christ and His Church if we are conversing with Him in prayer each day. Many of the spiritually indifferent Catholic men I have encountered are struggling in their prayer lives, and yet turning our thoughts to Him in prayer, thanking Him, and asking for His help can be so easy if we will only surrender and acknowledge that we can't do it alone.

One last thing. If we want to raise children who will remain faithful to Christ and His Church, they need to see fathers on their knees in prayer.

QUESTIONS FOR REFLECTION

1. Do I feel overwhelmed by prayer? Does breaking down my prayer life as the author suggested give me the encouragement that I can integrate meaningful prayer time into my life?
2. Can I think of times when I most needed to pray and did not? What would the result have been had I sought Christ's help or the intercession of our Blessed Mother?
3. In chapter one, the subject was the obstacles between men and Christ. Can I honestly expect to have a relationship with Jesus if I never talk to Him?
4. The idea of placing our prayer lives on our calendars was stressed by both the author and Dan Burke. In fact, I am encouraged to plan my prayer before anything else. Can I do this? Will I do this? Who will hold me accountable?

CHAPTER FIVE

Why Do We Follow a Secular Compass?

When I am weak and under the influence of
the surrounding culture, I tend to rely on myself
rather than the strength of Christ.
My prayer life is dry, I am unfocused in Mass,
and I am not grateful for the blessings in my life.
— Author —

I don't know about you, but I rarely get through the day without feeling beaten up a little by the demands and pervasive negative influence of the world. It is difficult to find peace and block out the noise. I am challenged to avoid committing the same venial sins over and over each day. In my weakness, I tend to rely on my own strength rather than Christ. These are the times I feel the farthest away from heaven. Does this ever happen to you?

In those quiet moments of self-reflection when nobody is around, I wonder if we acknowledge to ourselves (and God) our frequent tendency to blindly follow the secular compass offered by the world instead of the path that leads to heaven.

Just take a moment and consider how many times a day we are influenced to desire or buy something we don't need because of an advertisement or commercial. How often do we allow work and our pursuit of an illusory "better life" offered by modern culture divert us away from more meaningful time spent in prayer, investing in our families, or serving our communities. Do we sometimes try to fill the emptiness we feel inside with alcohol, drugs, sex, shopping, gambling, pornography, or a host of other sinful Band-Aids rather than seek the good and satisfying things Jesus has in store for us?

I am drawn again to the image of the secular compass and how it is leading us away from the heavenly home God wants for us. If we are honest, we will likely admit we allow this to happen through our pride, fear, ignorance, and lukewarmness. How do we get back on the right track?

First, let's have a reality check and be clear about the issues:

- The world offers *celebrities* to idolize—
  The Church offers *saints* to follow.
- The world offers *noise*—
  The Church offers *peace*.
- The world offers *false dreams*—
  The Church offers *truth*.
- The world offers and celebrates *vice*—
  The Church offers a life of *virtue*.
- The world offers *earthly pleasures*—
  The Church offers *eternal heaven*.

Second, we need to focus on taking clear and actionable steps to redirect our course. Here are five suggestions.

PRACTICE DETACHMENT

Reflect on the lessons in the last chapter from Fr. Connor and Tom Peterson. Let's ask ourselves if we really need "it," whatever "it" is. Let go of the material things that are in the way of our prayer lives, church attendance, charitable giving, volunteering, and certainly our relationships with Christ.

REMEMBER THE MASS IS ABOUT THE EUCHARIST

Have we prayed to be worthy to receive Jesus? Have we thanked God for this gift? Have we prayed to let others see Christ in us? Reverence, gratitude, humility, worship—these are the key words to remember about the Mass.

GO TO RECONCILIATION AS OFTEN AS POSSIBLE

Sin has weight. Every sin we commit in thought, word, or deed is transformed into a burdensome weight we carry around with us. Do a thorough and honest examination of conscience. Where have we fallen short? Confess these sins to a priest and be forgiven. We should go more frequently to the Sacrament of Reconciliation to confess our sins and make a sincere commitment not to have the same sins to confess each time.

BE COURAGEOUS

Men, our families are under attack! Watch any number of popular TV shows and you will see the diminished or ridiculed role of fathers and husbands. Our wives and children will pay a heavy price if we don't fight back against these stereotypes and be the leaders of our families we are called to be. We can either buy into the lies or have the courage to fight for those we love. Which will it be?

RECOGNIZE THE NEED FOR DAILY SURRENDER AND ONGOING CONVERSION

As I shared in chapter two, I learned early on in my faith journey that my surrender to God's will and subsequent conversion was *not* a one-time event. We must always put His will before our own and experience a daily "dying of self" in order for Christ to be in charge of our lives.

PURSUE HEAVEN, REJECT THE WORLD

Heaven is our ultimate destination and not this place called Earth. Will our critics help us get to heaven? Will they stand up for us during tough times? No, they will pull us into a secular way of life that has little room for God and where materialism and popularity are the fashionable idols of the day. Doing what is right is not always easy, but in the long run it is clearly the most beneficial. Why would we not choose heaven?

In today's hectic world, we are almost always moving and going somewhere, but are we going in the right direction? We will encounter obstacles to living out our faith, but we must be strong and overcome these challenges. If we are committed to following the six actions above and the guidance in the last chapter on prayer, let's also prayerfully consider enlisting the help of trusted friends to hold us accountable and speak truth into our lives. Remember our enemy and the prince of this world is the devil, and he will stop at nothing to keep us from Christ and our heavenly home.

St. Augustine once wrote:

> In former times, Christians were incited to renounce Christ; now they are taught to deny Christ. Then they were forced, now they are taught; then violence was used, now it is deception; then one heard the shouts

> of the Enemy; now, when he prowls around, gentle and insinuating, it is difficult to recognize him. Everyone knows how he tried to force Christians to deny Christ: he tried to attract them to himself so that they would renounce him; but they confessed Christ and were crowned by him. Now they are taught to deny Christ by trickery, because he doesn't want them to realize that he is drawing them away from Christ. (*Commentaries on the Psalms*, 39:1)

If this was the case in the fifth century, how much more true is it today?

As I was preparing to start the book and praying for discernment and the guidance of the Holy Spirit, I thought about this particular chapter a great deal. I kept coming back to the sacraments, particularly the Eucharist and Reconciliation, as the missing pieces for the Catholic men I frequently encounter who are struggling in their faith. With this in mind, I reached out to Father Dan Ketter, a priest who has long had my respect and admiration for his passion for sharing the truth of our Catholic faith and working with men's ministries.

After nine years in the healthcare information technology arena, Fr. Ketter entered the seminary to begin six years of formation for the priesthood in the Roman Catholic Church. Ordained in 2008, he served for four years as Parochial Vicar at St. Jude the Apostle Catholic Church and School in Sandy Springs, Georgia.

In the summer of 2012, Archbishop Wilton Gregory of the Archdiocese of Atlanta asked Fr. Ketter to begin a three-year program of study at The Catholic University of America in Washington, D.C. toward a Licentiate in Canon Law (JCL). Once completed Fr. Ketter will return to the Archdiocese of

Atlanta where he will serve on the Metropolitan Tribunal of the Archdiocese.

Father Ketter, you were very involved in the men's club at St. Jude the Apostle Catholic Church in Atlanta before beginning your graduate studies in canon law at the Catholic University of America. Have you always been passionate about helping Catholic men grow in their faith? Why?

> "Occasionally in the seminary we would get a semester break that afforded us the chance to steal away for a few days. One such break a few of us travelled home with one of our fellow seminarians whose family lived not too far from the seminary. Naturally on Sunday we all went to Mass together. It was a beautiful old church in a picturesque New England town. The Mass was fairly well attended and the priest gave a good homily. But what struck me the most about that experience was that other than the priest, every other person who carried out a liturgical role at that Mass was a female. The cantor was a woman, the two readers were women, the three altar servers were girls, every Extraordinary Minister of Holy Communion—I think there were four or five—was a woman. If it wouldn't have been so obvious I would have turned around to look into the choir loft to see if the organist was a woman.
>
> "There is nothing at all wrong with having women exercising these ministries, but I couldn't help but wonder, where the heck are all the men? It also made me ponder what kind of message such a scene sends to young and not-so-young boys sitting in the pews.

Quite possibly that message is, Church/religion and faith are 'girl things.'

"Though some will disagree with this statement, I think women more readily connect with the spiritual dimension of reality. Something about the way God made women enables them to more readily identify the whole order of reality that exists beyond the material world. They seem to have a kind of spiritual intuition. Please note that this is different than saying women are more spiritual than men. Objectively speaking, men and women are equally spiritual—both are given a spiritual soul directly by God; both are known and loved personally by God; both are made to be perfectly united with God in heaven for all eternity. Women however, it seems to me, have something of an intuitive sense of this, and as a result they more readily feel at home in spiritual contexts. Perhaps this is part of the feminine genius that St. Pope John Paul II wrote about during his pontificate.

"Again, this does not mean men are less spiritual or less able to cultivate a spiritual life. It just means that it takes more time to get them started, to get them moving forward and developing a comfort and confidence engaging in things spiritual. In light of this fact, I don't think it's helpful to present the faith to women and men in exactly the same way. What will speak to women will not necessarily speak to men and vice versa. Too often I think men are forgotten. We present the faith in a 'one-size-fits-all' fashion and figure that since it seems to work for many it must be sufficient for all. I think we need to do a better job providing opportunities for women and men to engage and grow in their faith separately, otherwise the men get left in the dust and then can easily check out spiritually.

"Scripture is clear that men in general, and husbands and fathers in particular, are to be the spiritual leaders. And spiritual leadership as Jesus defined it is not a leadership of dominance, power, or control, but leadership of sacrificial service. Men will be unable to carry out this role if they are feeling left behind or have checked out, and that is bad for all in the Church. Thus we need to do a better job of engaging men and helping them to recognize the spiritual part of themselves, to value it and cultivate its growth. The whole Church will be stronger as a result."

What are the biggest issues Catholic men face today in growing in their spiritual lives?

"As I mentioned, men don't connect to things spiritual as readily, and as a result can feel spiritually left in the dust by women. Men don't like feeling incompetent at something and when they do they avoid it—a matter related to pride, which I touch on below. So when men don't naturally or intuitively connect with their spiritual lives they will quickly give it up if they don't get some help. They will gravitate to things that they can more easily connect to—concrete, objective, measurable things. I think this is why sports and careers are so attractive to men. The objectives are very clear and it is very easy to measure how well you are doing. The problem is that our culture holds up these sorts of material things as the markers of success. Accumulating a lot of wealth, power, and status means that you are successful. So men end up giving an inordinate amount of time and energy to pursuing these things so as to shore up their sense of worth. Helping men to place a similar kind of priority on their spiritual lives is a big challenge. The move from what is concrete and measurable to what is spiritual and intangible is difficult. The move from what the world places so much value on to what much of the world values very little is difficult. We need to help them make this shift and begin to understand the value and importance of cultivating a strong spiritual life. We need to help them see that all things material will eventually pass away while all things spiritual will endure forever."

What keeps Catholic men from fully partaking of the sacramental life offered by the Church? Specifically, the Eucharist and Reconciliation?

"The Sacrament of Reconciliation is the forgotten sacrament. (I've heard it said in a tongue-in-cheek manner that Reconciliation is the best kept secret in the Church.) Pride and poor formation contribute to its neglect. As men we tend to be full of pride, and pride is perhaps the biggest obstacle to taking advantage of the Sacrament of Reconciliation. To confess to another human being all the ways you've failed demands the renunciation of pride, and for men this is no easy thing. (It's no easy thing for *anyone*, but particularly for men.) Who wants to acknowledge all their failures, let alone tell another person about them? Pride gives a man a hundred excuses why he doesn't need to go to Reconciliation. The antidote to the vice of pride, of course, is the virtue of humility. Every visit to the Sacrament of Reconciliation is a further leveling of pride and growth in humility. Men also avoid Reconciliation because, as several of our pontiffs have pointed out, we have lost the sense of sin. Catholics in general and Catholic men in particular don't understand the gravity of sin and therefore the importance of avoiding it at all costs and confessing it when they fail to do so. When a man begins to understand the seriousness of sin and what it does to his soul, to his relationship with God, and to the human community, he then begins to appreciate the value of Reconciliation.

"There is a similar problem with the Eucharist but it has a different effect. The similarity is poor formation and catechesis. Many men do not fully understand and appreciate the incredible gift Jesus has given us in the Eucharist. They do not understand what it means to receive the Eucharist and how to properly prepare themselves to receive it. The effect of this poor catechesis, this poor Eucharistic formation, is that many, many men come to the Eucharist poorly disposed to receive our Lord. The same amount of grace is offered us every time we receive the Eucharist, but how much of that grace we actually appropriate is dependent upon how well disposed we are. The solution, at least in part, is better Eucharistic formation. We must help men better understand the truth about the Eucharist and the incredible gift that it is—and the demands it makes upon us.

"Not incidentally, these two sacraments go together. The more a man avails himself of the Sacrament of Reconciliation the more well-disposed he is to receive the graces of the Eucharist. The more graces he receives in the Eucharist the more he will grow in self-knowledge. The more he grows in self-knowledge the more he will come to recognize his sins and his need for God's mercy and forgiveness, which will keep him coming back to Reconciliation."

What are the fruits of a sacramental life, especially for Catholic men?

"Grace! Grace is the very life of God, the very power of God within us. The vocation of husband and father is a difficult one. Being a Catholic man in today's world is difficult. On our own strength we are inclined to failure. With God's power, which comes to us through the grace of the sacraments, we can be victorious."

If you were addressing a group of Catholic men right now, what would you share with them in terms of priorities? The kind of example they must set for others? What the Church offers to help them on their journey?

"[S]eek first his kingdom and his righteousness, and all these things shall be yours as well (Matthew 6:33). But one might ask, 'Where is the kingdom of God?'

> The kingdom of God is not a place or thing but a person—Jesus Christ. Jesus is the kingdom of God in human flesh. He is the one we must seek. Men must make Him the highest priority in their lives. Doing so will not cause other people and other things in their lives to be neglected. Rather, making Jesus the highest priority will help men to appreciate the true value of those people and things. We resist committing ourselves totally to Jesus because we are afraid of what we will lose. The only way we lose is by not giving ourselves completely to Him. I recall what Pope Emeritus Benedict said at the Holy Mass inaugurating his pontificate in 2005:
>
> *If we let Christ into our lives, we lose nothing, nothing, absolutely nothing of what makes life free, beautiful and great. No! Only in this friendship are the doors of life opened wide. Only in this friendship is the great potential of human existence truly revealed. Only in this friendship do we experience beauty and liberation.*
>
> "What Jesus offers men is nothing less than Himself. Jesus gives Himself completely to those who say yes to His invitation of friendship. Jesus, *who came that we may have life, and have it abundantly* (John 10:10), causes men to experience the abundant life for which they were made and for which their hearts long. But in order for that to happen they must make Him the highest priority in their lives."

The choice is simple: heaven or this world. We can either spend our time thinking, speaking, and working with our focus on our heavenly home or wasting our energies chasing the temporary pleasures of this world. Deep in our hearts we must realize that the "secular compass" is not leading us down the right path. Prayer, detachment, courage, surrender, conversion, the Eucharist, and Reconciliation are the weapons at our disposal to fight the secular culture and embrace heaven. Are we using them?

If not, begin now. A great help to you would be to *register* at your parish and make an appointment to go and meet the pastor. Sit down and talk to him. Get to know him and help him get to know you and your family. All you need to say is, "Father, I would like to live a more intentionally Catholic life. Can you help me?" This will pay immense dividends!

QUESTIONS FOR REFLECTION

1. As I reflect on this chapter, have I fallen into the trap of following the "secular compass"? Can I think of specific times in my life when I have done so?
2. One of the key themes of this book is a wakeup call to men about pursuing heaven and not this world. Do I make decisions on a daily basis through the filter of what will help me get to heaven or do I focus more on what will make my short time on earth more enjoyable?
3. Father Ketter describes Reconciliation as the "forgotten sacrament." Having read his thoughts and review of Church teaching, do I go to

Reconciliation with the frequency I should? What is holding me back?

4. Father Ketter makes it clear, based on Scripture, that men are to be the spiritual leaders in their homes. Am I the spiritual leader in my home? Do I make going to Mass, to Confession, and simply being a Catholic look attractive and inviting to my loved ones? Do I want them to follow the example I am currently setting?

CHAPTER SIX

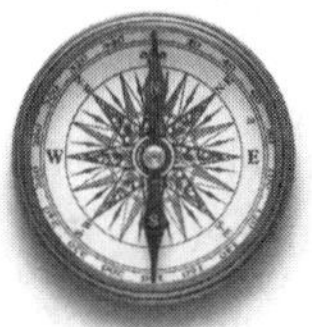

Relying on Our Brothers in Christ

It took me surrendering to Christ and letting go
of my emotionally walled-off old self to recognize
how much I needed to have Catholic brothers in my life.
— Author —

"I am a rock. I am an island." These words from an old Simon and Garfunkel song sum up how I viewed the need for close friendships for most of my life. The stubbornness and pride that had led me to walk away from the Baptist Church as a teenager had manifested themselves as a formidable wall around my heart and a reflexive need to keep others at an emotional distance. I was self-sufficient and thought I had it all figured out as I was growing my career after college and focused on work and little else. Then I met my wife in my late twenties and the wall around my heart began to crumble as I started sharing my life with someone I loved.

Although these were still my pre-Catholic years in the spiritual wilderness, I can look back and see my marriage and enduring love for my wife as the first steps in God's efforts to bring me back to a relationship with Him. When each of my sons were born, the wall around my heart eroded further and continued steadily until the fall of 2005 when I experienced a profound conversion to Christ. I wrote extensively about my conversion to the Catholic Church in my second book *Along the Way: Lessons for An Authentic Journey of Faith*, and won't devote much time to it here. What is important is to recognize that I came to the place when the wall around my heart was largely gone after years of the Holy Spirit and my unconditional love for my family working on me. I surrendered to Christ and stopped trying to compete with Him for control. I gave up everything to Him and received back everything I needed (not necessarily what I might have wanted). I went from saying no to God for over two decades to saying yes, and that has had an incredible impact on my life and family.

So, what does this have to do with friendship?

After I surrendered to Christ and began RCIA to enter the Catholic Church on the Feast of Christ the King in 2006, I began experiencing a need for friendship with other Catholic men and a desire to end my self-imposed lonely exile. I sought out husbands, fathers, and business people in my parish community who I could go to for help and, in turn, I could help as well. It took me surrendering to Christ and letting go of my emotionally walled-off old self to recognize how much I needed to have Catholic brothers in my life. My surrender came from a place of humility and the recognition that I was *not* self-sufficient. I needed people outside of my immediate family to help and encourage me on the journey in front of me. I also needed a group of friends to be brutally honest with me and help me stay on the right track.

In 2007 I formed a group of Catholic businessmen with the help of Deacon Mike Bickerstaff. The goal was to gather together once a month with like-minded Catholic men from the Atlanta business community who wanted to more fully integrate their faith with their work. Many of those men are still in the group and we have added others over the years. We come together for prayer, a Gospel reflection, and talk through topics relevant to living out our faith at work and the public square. The group often does service projects together where we involve our families. We also have very candid conversations and open sharing built on trust and the knowledge that we will keep the conversations confidential and not judge each other. I value these conversations more than I can ever express with the written word.

This group of men is my bedrock. I can count on them and they, in turn, can count on me. I get honesty, encouragement, support, and every now and then a well-deserved kick in the pants from these great men. These are my brothers in Christ and I am grateful for them. The Church, parishes, and many other organizations offer a number of good options for Catholic men seeking friendship and brotherhood. One such organization is the Knights of Columbus. I am an inactive Second Degree Knight, primarily because of the weeknight schedule with my sons and their activities, but I love the mission of the Knights of Columbus and everything they stand for. Because of my admiration for the Knights, I reached out to Brian Caulfield to get his thoughts on the importance of friendship and brotherhood for Catholic men.

Brian is the editor of the website FathersforGood.org, sponsored by the Knights of Columbus Supreme Council, and is a communications specialist in the Office of the Supreme Knight in New Haven, Connecticut. Since December 2011 he also has served as Vice Postulator of the Cause for Canonization of Father Michael McGivney, the founder of the Knights of Columbus who holds the title of Venerable. Brian served as editor of the book *Man to Man, Dad to Dad: Catholic Faith and Fatherhood* (Pauline, 2013).

Brian, I have long appreciated the wonderful ministry work you do for Catholic men through your work with the Knights of Columbus and your FathersforGood.org website. I am curious to capture your thoughts on the need for fellowship and encouragement among Catholic men. Why is this so important?

> "Men face a number of challenges in today's culture but the most basic involve questions about the very nature of manhood and masculinity. For decades, men, in particular fathers, have been portrayed in popular media as clueless and often dangerous. In television and movies, if Dad isn't being led around by his wise wife and hoodwinked by his wise-guy children, then it's likely that he's a macho philanderer or even an abuser. I generalize, of course, but there is a definite trend in this direction.
>
> "Add to this the fact that over the same decades there has been an increase of broken homes and children

losing contact with their divorced father, and you have a crisis of manhood and fatherhood.

"So, yes, men have a special need these days to bond in fellowship with other men. They need to be fathered and mentored, they need to feel comfortable in their masculinity among other men and accepted by them. Of course, this is a goal of the organization I work for, the Knights of Columbus, but there are other men's movement groups that guys can look to."

What are the obstacles keeping Catholic men from relying on each other for support and help in excelling in our faith, at home, and at work?

"Well, there's a trust factor. Guys are famous for not being comfortable with 'sharing' at least on an emotional level. But there are many guy activities that bring men together—watching sports, playing sports, talking cars, tools, and gadgets. Yet so much of a man's time today is centered around family life, if he's married, because men are expected to pull a fair share of child care and household chores. This is a good thing because it supports the most important bond of a husband with his wife. But it also discourages the type of man to man sharing and bonding that can be healthy for masculine development. I think the answer is for husband and wife to discuss a guy's need to reach out and bond with other men in order to become a better husband and father, and a guy's need to lead as spiritual head of the family, as dynamic worker and breadwinner and authority figure with the children.

I may be wrong, but I think if husband and wife have an honest and trustful discussion, they can work out a healthy balance that is so vital for marriage."

For the shy or nervous Catholic man interested in connecting with other Catholic brothers in his parish or local community but is not sure how to do it, what would be your advice?

"Even shy guys can volunteer, show up, and get the job done. Guys relate by working together, testing one another, supporting one another, and if a shy guy works hard and is reliable, he will be accepted."

Can you share an example from your own life or the life of someone you know where the impact of Catholic brotherhood made a significant difference?

"In my experience with the Knights of Columbus, I have seen faith and fraternity in action. Perhaps the most notable example can be seen after 9/11, when the nation was reeling from shock and horror over the terrorist attacks that took so many lives. The Knights responded a few days later with the Heroes Fund, which provided three thousand dollars in immediate emergency funds to the families of fallen firefighters and police officers, the first responders who went to their death trying to save others. The checks were delivered to widows personally by the Knights of Columbus insurance agents. It didn't matter if the deceased hero was a Knight or even a Catholic. In so many cases, the funds were the first tangible relief these families had in a tragic situation. It was a great example of what Catholic brotherhood can do."

Friendship, brotherhood, fellowship, male bonding, accountability, prayer, spiritual growth, service, these are the words which come to mind when I think of how important it is for me to have other Catholic men in my life. How about you? So many other men I know and respect are much better at this idea of Catholic brotherhood than me, and I am grateful for their example. But other men I have observed struggle with this concept. They do not participate in parish-based events or meetings or join the men-focused groups available to them. In fact, they are rarely seen outside of weekly Mass. Why?

I have been able to glean some insight from a few of these men I have gotten to know and through simple observation. Here is what I have learned.

A FEW MEN SHARED THAT THEY DIDN'T FEEL WELCOMED BY THE GROUPS

This is a legitimate concern. For those of us already in groups or organizations, we have an absolute obligation to make everyone feel welcomed, no question.

SOME MEN ARE SIMPLY SHY AND INTROVERTED

Fair enough. Maybe the way to take the first steps is to volunteer for a service project within the parish. As Brian Caulfield shared, showing up and helping out can gain fast acceptance from other men. You don't have to be the life of the party to participate, just work on being comfortable around your Catholic brothers.

"I AM BUSY AND DON'T HAVE TIME"

I hear this a lot. Everyone has a different situation, but ask yourself if you are missing something in your life. Do you ever have a desire to speak to other men who have similar backgrounds and experiences? Are we using our families as an excuse? I am guilty of this at times, but I try to bring my sons to service projects whenever possible and this has been a good compromise.

"MY EVENINGS ARE FOR FAMILY"

Great, so are mine. We all understand, especially if our kids are under the age of eighteen. Why not focus on breakfast or lunch meetings? There are plenty of Catholic men's Bible studies and prayer groups which meet during these times. At the very least, make an attempt to meet other parishioners and get together one on one. Just make the effort and the payoff will be tremendous.

The biggest objection I heard was, "I don't see the point." If this is your take on the idea of Catholic brotherhood, let me push back a little. Is your faith life where you want it to be? How is your prayer life? Are you still growing as a Catholic man and, if so, who are your role models? Wouldn't it be a relief to be able to discuss your challenges and struggles with other men who get it and can offer sound advice? Do you have all of the encouragement and prayers you could ever want? Are your current relationships aiding you—or hindering you—on your journey to holiness and relationship with Jesus? I think you get the point. Men need other men. *Iron sharpens iron, and one man sharpens another* (Proverbs 27:17).

What if Jesus came into the world and never chose the Apostles? Who would have carried on in evangelizing the world after the Ascension? Who would have recruited other men to take their places? We are called to be holy, we are called to evangelize, and we are made for heaven. The journey will be much more enjoyable and fruitful in the company of our brothers.

QUESTIONS FOR REFLECTION

1. Do I know any of the men in my parish or larger Catholic community? If so, how much time do I spend with them?
2. Can I buy into the idea that becoming part of a parish group for men or other Catholic men's organization can enrich my faith, my prayer life, and help me grow as a man? What is holding me back?
3. The author wrote about the importance of accountability among men. Who holds me accountable in my prayer life, spiritual life, family life, and challenges me to grow and improve?
4. Brian Caulfield shared the importance of having a candid dialogue with our wives about the need for reasonable, guilt-free bonding time with other men. Have I had this discussion with my wife (if married)? If not, am I willing?

PART II

FAMILY

CHAPTER SEVEN

On Marriage, Leadership, and Honoring Our Wives

Honoring our wives, which not surprisingly
is also one of the best things we can do for our children,
requires us to slow down, pay attention, listen, and
be truly present.
— Joel Schmidt —

Marriage is in trouble everywhere, especially in our country with over half of marriages ending in divorce. Our culture, so influenced by Hollywood and materialism, has set about creating a society which no longer values marriage and the family in favor of one which glorifies selfishness, greed, and offers false idols for us to worship instead of God. As an author and speaker I attempt to reach people with Christ-inspired work, which will help them lead authentic and integrated Catholic lives. Many of us are called to other roles in the world that require great courage and effort, but I suggest nothing will do more to strengthen marriage and the family than men having the courage to reject the surrounding culture and embrace their roles as loving husbands, faith-filled fathers, and leaders in our homes.

Is it possible that marriage and the family are losing their value in the eyes of the next generation because our young people don't see enough good alternative examples of successful marriages and Christ-centered families? If we truly offered this alternative and fought to live it, defend it, and promote it, there could be a resurgence of successful marriages, more children being born, and parishes packed with faithful Catholic families. What will it take? Men must lead.

Everything you learned in the Faith section of this book has prepared you for what you are about to read. Men, we must reject the lies of the culture, let go of our idols, get rid of the obstacles between us and Christ, pray faithfully, and accept the call to holiness we received at our baptism. We are not here to indulge ourselves in a world of moral relativism and personal pleasure, but instead to create Christ-centered homes, raise our children to love God, and help each other to attain heaven.

Feeling overwhelmed? This is a tall order and this would be an understandable response. However, the alternative is further disintegration of marriage and the family—and the next casualties could be our own if we neglect our responsibilities. Is there anyone who can help us? Look no further than our wives.

The first time I met my wife over twenty years ago I knew she was the one for me. It was a strange feeling of excitement, nervousness, certainty, and peace all mixed together. As the years have passed and we have faced the roller coaster ride of life together, I still experience that same feeling from time to time. I am blessed and I thank God for placing her in my life. We don't have a perfect marriage (who does?), but we have a successful marriage and the fruit of it can be seen in our sons, in the fact that we love each other as much we did in our younger days and in the faith-filled home we have made together.

My wife and I are a team and we understand our vocation as parents is to get each other and our children to heaven. We also understand our roles and know what each of us is responsible for in achieving goals for our family. My wife challenges me and helps me grow as a man, a husband, a father, and most certainly in my spiritual life as a Catholic. She keeps my pride and ego in check, reminds me when I get off track, and her quiet but passionate faith inspires me. In fact, it was my wife's interest in the Catholic Church in 2005 that was a critical catalyst for our family joining the Church a year later.

What is so important about marriage? The Catechism of the Catholic Church teaches us that the Sacrament of Marriage is a "covenant," a "partnership," and "ordered toward the good of the spouses" (1601). We learn further that "'the intimate community of life and love which constitutes the married state has been established by the Creator and endowed by him with its own proper laws. . . . God himself is the author of marriage' [GS 48, no.1]. The vocation to marriage is written in the very nature of man and woman as they came from the hand of the Creator" (1603). We understand that "man is created in the image and likeness of God who is himself love [Cf. Gen 1:27; 1 Jn 4:8, 16]. Since God created him man and woman, their mutual love becomes an image of the absolute and unfailing love with which God loves man. It is good, very good, in the Creator's eyes" (1604).

Most importantly, the Catechism states: "Holy Scripture affirms that man and woman were created for one another: 'It is not good that the man should be alone' [Gen 2:18]. The woman, 'flesh of his flesh,' his equal, his nearest in all things, is given to him by God as a 'helpmate'; she thus represents God from whom comes our help [Gen 2:18–25]. 'Therefore a man leaves his father and his mother and cleaves to his wife, and they become one flesh' [Gen 2:24]. The Lord himself shows that this signifies an unbreakable union of their two lives by recalling what the plan of the Creator had been 'in the beginning': 'So they are no longer two, but one flesh'" (1605).

What we can glean from that is very important. God has sent our wives to us and us to our wives to assist each other in our relationships with Him and our journey to heaven. Let us consider a few important questions:

- Do we truly see our wives in this light? Do we actively seek their help?
- If asked, would our wives describe themselves as our "partners" in life?
- What keeps us from seeking or accepting this help? Is it pride? Ego? Misunderstanding the role our wives play? The roles we play?
- Do we love our wives and treat them as a gift from God?
- Do our children and friends look at us and see the example of a loving and faith-filled marriage centered in Christ?

As we ponder these convicting questions and our response, let us also consider practical ideas and actions for how we can best be the leaders we are called to be, honor our wives, and have blessed marriages.

1. **Thankfulness to God, gratefulness to our wives.** It can be easy to take our loves ones for granted, especially our wives. Do we thank our wives for all that they do and mean to us? Do our children know how much we love, honor, and appreciate our wives, and are we inspiring them to do the same one day in their own families? Do we thank God each day for giving us the gift of our wives? "Authentic conjugal love presupposes and requires that a man have a profound respect for the equal dignity of his wife: 'You are not her master' . . . 'but her husband; she was not given you to be your slave, but your wife. . . . Reciprocate her attentiveness to you and be grateful to her for her love'" (St. Pope John Paul II, *Familiaris Consortio*).

2. **Get our priorities in order.** Christ first, family second, work third. If Christ is not first in our lives then we are lost. One of the reasons for the breakdown of the family is that we spend too much time competing with Him for control. I lived that life for over twenty years and it wasn't until I put my pride aside and surrendered to Christ in 2005 that I began to understand that I couldn't fully love my wife and children in the way they deserved until I acknowledged Christ as first in my life. "Today we can no longer be Christians as a simple consequence of the fact that we live in a society that has Christian roots: even those born to a Christian family and formed in the faith must, each and every day, renew the choice to be a Christian, to give God first place, before the temptations continuously suggested by a secularized culture, before the criticism of many of our contemporaries" (Pope Benedict XVI, Wednesday Audience, February 13, 2013).

3. View marriage as an apostolate and a blessed mission. "Christian couples should be aware that they are called to sanctity themselves and to sanctify others, that they are called to be apostles and that their first apostolate is in the home. They should understand that founding a family, educating their children, and exercising a Christian influence in society, are supernatural tasks. The effectiveness and the success of their life—their happiness—depends to a great extent on their awareness of their specific mission" (St. Josemaria Escriva, *Conversations with St. Josemaria Escriva,* Scepter Publishers, 2008, 91).

4. Be the spiritual leader in our homes. This is not a competition. Men too often sit on the sidelines and wives take on this role while we remain detached and disengaged. We should again thank God for our wives, but *we* are called to be spiritual leaders and not narrowly view our roles as only the financial providers. Remember what Father Ketter shared in chapter five? "Scripture is clear that men in general, and husbands and fathers in particular, are to be the spiritual leaders. And spiritual leadership as Jesus defined it is not a leadership of dominance, power, or control, but leadership of sacrificial service." The positive impact on our marriages and the faith lives of our children is beyond measure.

Just like evangelizing to others can only be accomplished by a sincere, joy-filled sharing of the Good News and setting a good example, making marriage more attractive will only be accomplished by the world seeing more men and women committed to love, selflessness, humility, sacrifice, courage, and devotion to Christ. It seems to me that one of the most important and enduring legacies my wife and I can give to our children and the rest of the world is a successful example of a Christ-centered marriage. One such Catholic couple who have long held my admiration and respect is Joel and Lisa Schmidt. I was keen on interviewing Joel for this chapter because of the example he sets for other Catholic men and the great advice he and his wife share on their website, ThePracticingCatholic.com.

Joel, thank you for taking the time to be interviewed for my new book. For readers who are not familiar with you, can you share a brief bio?

> "Absolutely. Lisa and I have been married for nine years and have three children, so far: Lucy, five; Jude, almost two; and Lydia, one month. We are in the final year of diaconate formation, with me scheduled to be ordained in August 2014. We are also developing a ministry in conjunction with our local diocese to provide support to couples who have experienced miscarriage, stillbirth, and infant loss. In addition, we write for various Catholic websites including our own, ThePracticingCatholic.com, which is our personal blog about attempting to live a joy-filled Catholic life. Finally, we speak to Catholic groups, primarily about marital and family spirituality. Professionally, I have a PhD in biochemistry and work as a research scientist."

Joel, I have long respected the way you and your wife Lisa live your lives, and your marriage is a great example to us all. What is the key to a happy Catholic marriage?

> "Permanence. 'Will you love and honor each other as man and wife for the rest of your lives?' In the

wedding rite, you actually have to promise to do that. You don't get to enter into marriage with conditions. Our sponsor couple did a good job of driving that point home during our marriage preparation. They told us that the primary thing that will keep a couple together and ultimately make a marriage successful is not love; it's commitment. There will be days when you don't feel very loving toward each other, which is natural; feelings come and go. Other friends once told us, 'No matter what's going on, whatever we might be fighting about, the marriage is never on the line. That's just understood.'

"The meaning of 'for better or worse' is difficult to truly grasp without understanding marriage as a sacrament. It really makes no sense to stick two selfish, wounded, sinful people together and expect them to stay together forever, so there has to be something else at work. God's grace poured out through the Sacrament of Marriage can transform those two people from self-serving to self-sacrificing. Husband and wife both have to be willing to empty themselves for the good of the other. It takes real courage to be vulnerable enough to hold nothing back for yourself, which is only possible if you know the other person is not heading for the exit at the first sign of trouble. You have to know you'll still be loved when you make mistakes."

Are there difficult days in the Schmidt house? How do you and Lisa cope with the inevitable challenges of marriage and raising children?

"Nope. Well okay, maybe a few. It's a common cliché to say that marriage should be a 50-50 partnership, but that's simply wrong. It has to be 100-100, with both husband and wife at any given time being willing to invest everything they have, holding nothing back. When things get tense, you have to come together rather than apart. Lisa and I are at our worst whenever we begin to turn on each other. When arguments ensue, returning fire is not justified just because the other person shot first. Instead of retreating and becoming selfish, you have to give more in understanding and charity.

"Another excellent piece of advice we got from our sponsor couple is never to argue about the details of what was said that led to a conflict. Both of you will be convinced you're right ('I know what I said,' or 'I know what I heard'), so there's no possible resolution. Agree to disagree and figure out how to move forward together. This keeps the focus on unified problem solving rather than finger-pointing and blaming."

Clearly, you and Lisa honor the Sacrament of Marriage. What is your advice to other Catholic men out there on how to do the same?

"Speak well of each other, always. After all, you married each other. Guys, if your wife is such a shrew, what does that say about you? If you constantly complain about your wife, it just makes you look stupid and small. When people around you are degrading their wives by talking them down, don't participate. These opportunities to practice the virtues of prudence and charity will eventually begin to permeate your interactions with your wife. You might be surprised what it does for your attitude toward her and your marriage overall.

"You don't have to pretend that everything is always sunshine and rainbows, but there's no need to air your martial struggles in public either. The need to 'let off steam' is a myth; remember that steam burns whoever comes into contact with it. Note, this is not the same as discussing a genuine problem with a trusted confidant. 'Venting' may relieve the pressure for a while, but it does nothing to change the conditions giving rise to it. If something in your marriage is causing such a negative, heated reaction inside you, you owe it to your wife to take it to prayer to discern why and then work it out privately with her."

Do you think men struggle with "honoring" their wives? Is there a pride issue or a fear of giving up control that men find difficult to overcome?

"It has been said that 'idle hands are the devil's workshop,' but overly busy hands can be dangerous, too. One of the devil's cleverest devices is keeping people, men in particular, busy. This is often under the guise of doing good, like providing for his wife and family. There is tremendous societal and peer pressure to do this. The man who provides material abundance for his family is almost universally revered without considering what his family really needs.

Perhaps they need less stuff and more of him. They may need him to 'do' less and 'be' more.

"Honoring our wives, which not surprisingly is also one of the best things we can do for our children, requires us to slow down, pay attention, listen, and be truly present. In a sense this requires us to give up control because we have to respond rather than always initiating. Success is neither predictable nor objectively measurable, and the return on investment is seldom immediate. However, the best way for a man to honor his wife is to earnestly strive to be the man she deserves, the man God is calling him to be. Men struggle with this because it is inherently just that, a struggle."

Joel, what impact does a vibrant prayer life and actively practicing our Catholic faith have on a marriage? What has been your own experience?

"Actively practicing the Catholic faith keeps Christ at the center of our marriage. This may sound trite, but it is a deep, rich truth that permeates every aspect of our relationship. It reminds us that our marriage is an analogy for the relationship between Christ and the Church. Every man should read Ephesians 5 and pay special attention to the husband's responsibilities. 'Husbands, love your wives, even as Christ loved the church and handed himself over for her.' If you want to know exactly what that means, look long and hard at a crucifix, because that's the level of sacrifice and service to which you're being called. That's why you

> need to spend a lot of time on your knees begging Jesus to pour out the grace of the sacrament in your heart.
>
> "Most men have no trouble stating unequivocally that they would take a bullet for their wives. However, that's easy, because most of us will never have to do that. The sacrifices actually required of us are usually smaller and more subtle but no less important. Can you skip watching that football game to go shopping for the kids' outfits for family pictures next week? Can you paint an entire room coral just because she needs to see it, knowing full well you'll be painting over it later? Can you give up the regular poker game with your college buddies with whom you now have nothing in common in lieu of a regular date night? Can you take the kids as soon as you walk in the door at the end of a long work day, because she's been home with them all day and needs a break? Can you love her heroically every day? You've got to beg Jesus for the grace to do it."

My brothers, we have a special and distinct role as Christian men, fathers, husbands, and leaders in the family, in the Church, and in society at large. If we don't step up, we run the risk of seeing our families overrun and absorbed by the surrounding culture. This is not acceptable. Start with prayer. Be faithful, be consistent, have courage, show humility, and remember . . . we are made for a heavenly home and not this world.

QUESTIONS FOR REFLECTION

1. The author challenges us to be the spiritual leaders in our homes. Am I leading or following, or apathetically sitting on the sidelines when it comes to spiritual leadership?
2. Do I do a good job of thanking my wife for all that she does for me and my family? Do I thank God for my wife? If not, what is holding me back?
3. Joel Schmidt shared that the "best way for a man to honor his wife is to earnestly strive to be the man she deserves, the man God is calling him to be." Am I trying to be the man God is calling me to be?
4. Joel also stated the old cliché of marriage being a 50-50 partnership is wrong, and that it should be 100-100 with "both husband and wife at any given time being willing to invest everything they have, holding nothing back." Do I understand and believe in the 100-100 concept that I must give everything I have to my marriage, as must my wife? Do I actually live this way?

CHAPTER EIGHT

Dads, Do We Have Our Acts Together?

It is easier for a father to have children than
for children to have a real father.
— Pope John XXIII —

During a coffee meeting with a friend not long ago, he said, "You seem to have your act together on the fatherhood front. What's your secret?" I was surprised and taken aback because I don't think I have my act together at all. I don't mean that out of false humility. I pray every day to be a better husband and father because I know all of the areas where I fall short. Before I could answer my friend, he received a call on his cell phone and had to run. The topic, however, stayed on my mind and was the impetus for this chapter.

What does "having your act together" as a Catholic father really mean? I'm not the expert, but it seems that this sort of father likely has his priorities straight with Christ first, family second, and work third. This kind of dad spends *quality* time with his family, not just time. This man is a role model to his family in living out his Catholic faith and being the light of Christ to others. This father has joy in his heart and is a man of prayer. This Catholic dad honors and loves his wife and lifts up the Sacrament of Marriage in the eyes of his children as something special and sacred. This sort of father finds in St. Joseph, the Patron Saint of Fathers, the ideal role model for how to serve God and his family.

What sort of rules or maxims might this Catholic father, who has his act together, follow to stay on the right path? If we consider what Scripture and the Church teach us, we can look to these four points as our guide.

1. Our vocation is to get our families to heaven.
2. Our children are always watching us. They will likely model later in life what they learn at home.
3. We are made for heaven, not this world. Let's act accordingly.
4. Our children are God's gift to us. The love and care we show our children is our gift back to Him.

Feeling convicted? Me too.

So, why did my friend say what he did over coffee? I believe he knows that I *try* to be a good father despite my numerous failings. He sees that I keep at it and don't give up. He knows that I constantly pray for guidance and help. I don't really have my act together, but I do sincerely believe failing as a dad is not an option because my children would ultimately pay the price if I am not successful in my vocation as a father and husband.

"It is easier for a father to have children than for children to have a real father" (Pope John XXIII).

Guess what, dads? Sometimes, you and I simply have to try harder. We have to give our best, even when we don't feel like it. We have to sacrifice some work time, fun time, down time, and me time for the sake of our families. It would be wise (although scary) for us to realize that our kids watch our every move and they will be like us one day. I pray that is a good thing.

Dads, I encourage all of us to take the four points listed above to prayer. Let's not allow our pride to keep us from asking for help. Seek the intercession of the Blessed Mother and St. Joseph. Let's pray for each other, challenge each other, and encourage each other. Let's live out our vocation to fatherhood with courage and honor, for as Archbishop Gomez of Los Angeles said, "It's a promise to be faithful to the vocation of being a father. Even after a long day of work, even if he'd rather be doing something else—instead he will smile and laugh and take delight in spending time and playing games with his kids. Because that's what fathers do. They keep their promise to love."

In the absence of us stepping up to our commitment as fathers, what are the alternatives? What can happen? After reflection and prayer, it seems obvious to me that most fathers likely face the same choices:

We can relinquish our fatherly responsibilities to others. We can allow peers, TV, the Internet, video games, and a godless materialistic culture to raise our children and just hope for the best.

OR

We can live up to our responsibilities and our vocation as fathers. We are called to be holy and our clear vocation is to help our family get to heaven. That is a tall order and requires courage, hard work, difficult choices, and lots of prayer.

How often do we say we want the second choice, but lose focus, get busy, and allow the first option to occur? I am afraid it happens all too often if we are honest with ourselves.

What can we do to make the second option the automatic choice? None of us are perfect, but perhaps we can follow these five basic steps to stay on course.

MAKE THE MOST OF OUR TIME TOGETHER

My younger son and I have been having great conversations on the way to lacrosse practice and when we throw the football in our front yard. My older son and I take long walks together for our best conversations. The important thing is to maximize every minute with our children as opportunities to share and guide them to good decisions in life. Making family dinner time a priority is one way to help make this happen. Know that efforts to get our attention are often potential cries for help. Our kids need us, but are we available?

LISTEN BEFORE LECTURING

This is difficult for me! The fastest way to have my sons clam up is for me to cut them off with a "coaching moment." I can coach later, but I need to hear them out first and encourage them to share their thoughts.

BE GREAT CATHOLIC ROLE MODELS

It doesn't get more basic than this, but do we realize how often our children are watching our every move? They will love God, be excited about Mass, and have devotion to our Catholic faith if we do. They will likely pray faithfully if we do. They will be more likely to grow up following the magisterium and staying out of the "Catholic cafeteria line" if we do.

HONOR THE SACRAMENT OF MARRIAGE

Want to see our children get married and start great families some day? As I shared in the last chapter, love our spouses and model the kind of marriage we want them to enjoy. Show open affection, say "I love you," and make sure the kids know how much we honor and respect the person we have married. We are dooming our kids to a marriageless future or possible divorce if they grow up in a home where the Sacrament of Marriage is not treasured and valued.

TUNE OUT POPULAR CULTURE AND "DETACH"

Guess what? As we covered in chapter three, if we are obsessed with American Idol, buying junk we don't need, and trying to keep up with the neighbors, our kids are likely to grow up emulating our behavior. I am beginning to feel that every minute spent in front of the TV or the computer is wasted time and a missed opportunity to interact with the family. This may be the hardest thing on the list, but we can do a better job with our time and focus.

Seeking more insight into the role and vocation of Catholic fathers, I reached out to Bishop Michael Sheridan of the Diocese of Colorado Springs. I first met Bishop Sheridan in 2012 when I was a speaker at the Colorado Springs Men's Conference and was impressed with his strong support for men's ministries. He was kind enough to share his thoughts on the subject of men and their vocation for this book.

Bishop Sheridan, what is the vocation of Catholic men? What are we called to do?

"The vocation of Catholic men is the same as for all people. It is the vocation of holiness. More particularly, men (especially married men) have the vocation to be an expression of God the Father's love, solicitude, and protection."

What are the obstacles that come between men and this vocation? How can we overcome them?

"The main obstacle, as I see it, is the refusal of our feminized culture to attribute this role to men. As a result, many men are simply not formed to take up their special vocation. Or they are afraid that, if they do, they will not be accepted by their peers."

Bishop Sheridan, I know you actively support men's ministries in your diocese. In fact, you and I met through the 2012 Colorado Springs Men's Conference. What role can these types of ministries, support groups, prayer groups, and conferences play in helping men realize and faithfully live out their vocation?

"Men can be both educated and energized by occasional conferences such as these. Of great importance, however, is creating the mechanisms that will enable them to gather with other men on a regular basis. Parish-based 'follow-up' groups are very important."

As you consider the Catholic men you encounter each day, what do you find encouraging? What gives you concern?

"My greatest encouragement comes from young men. It seems that many of them are not as afraid as their fathers might be to be formed as genuine Catholic 'fathers,' whether married or not. That having been said, I am greatly encouraged by those men who have discerned a vocation to the diaconate. This calls men to real signs of contradiction in our secularized and feminized culture. I am concerned only that we are not working hard enough to call men to real holiness. I don't worry about that, though. It's God's work. But we must not fail to be His instruments in every way that we can."

If you were speaking to a group of Catholic men, both single and married, what would you most like to say to them? What would you encourage them to do?

"If I had one shot at them, I guess I would speak to them about the universal call to holiness. It all starts there, no matter what one's particular vocation or circumstances of life might be. I don't think we have a very good appreciation of that call and how to live it out. I would encourage them to come to know God, especially the Father, better through prayerful reading of Scripture and wholehearted participation in the sacramental life of the Church."

Bishop Sheridan stated it as simply as possible: we have received the universal call to holiness and it all starts there, no matter what our vocation or circumstances might be. Will we respond to the call? Are we prepared to be the fathers our children deserve? Will we do everything we can to help them and our wives get to heaven?

Guys, doesn't being a better father feel like a wrestling match that never ends! This subject often comes up in my daily prayers as I seek discernment and courage to do the right things. The alternative to my daily struggle is to be apathetic, which will virtually guarantee that my children will grow up drifting without a good foundation of faith, values, and a sense of what is truly important in life. Kids are like clay looking to be formed and developed. In our absence, those who only see our children as consumers or who seek to do them harm will step into the vacuum.

Remember the fourth point stated earlier in the chapter?

Children are God's gift to us.
Taking excellent care of His creation is our gift back to Him

QUESTIONS FOR REFLECTION

1. Have I truly considered my vocation as a father before?
2. Do I allow less important things to come between me and time with my family? Am I usually present for them? If not, why not?
3. Am I a good Catholic role model for my children? Are they more or less likely to be good adult Catholics some day because of my influence?
4. Am I committed and ready to get my act together as a Catholic dad? Who will hold me accountable?

CHAPTER NINE

St. Joseph is the Model

Saint Joseph was a just man, a tireless worker,
the upright guardian of those entrusted to his care.
May he always guard, protect and enlighten families.
— St. Pope John Paul II —

As the father of a teenager with high-functioning autism, I am sometimes challenged to give my oldest child the focus and patience he needs from me. I frequently feel inadequate when I advise and guide my younger son through the minefields of today's culture. My loving wife should expect my best efforts as a husband, yet I often feel distracted or too worn out to give her the 100 percent she deserves. What can we do when it becomes obvious that we need to make a course correction and get back on track?

Shortly after I entered the Church I recall a Mass when I lingered a few minutes to ask for the intercession and help of St. Joseph. It was the first time I sought the assistance of this great saint and my devotion to him has grown over the years. As a Catholic dad and husband, who better for me to emulate than the patron saint of fathers? I have long been drawn to St. Joseph and find in his life the encouragement to be more obedient and trusting in God's promises. Even though I often wrestle with self-created challenges on the parenting and marriage fronts, my shortcomings are somewhat lessened and I feel encouraged to do better when I pray for his intercession and reflect on his courageous example in caring for Jesus and Mary.

When I reflect on St. Joseph's life and seek his help, I find myself quickly getting back on track with my family responsibilities and regaining the peace that frequently leaves me when I allow work and the pressures of the world to dominate my thoughts and calendar. Here are five important lessons I have learned from St. Joseph as I have addressed my struggles over the years.

FIVE LESSONS FROM ST. JOSEPH

1. St. Joseph was *obedient*. Joseph was obedient to God's will throughout his life. Joseph listened to the angel of the Lord explain the virgin birth in a dream and not to be afraid to take Mary, his wife, into his home (Matthew 1:20–24). He was obedient when he led his family to Egypt to escape Herod's infanticide in Bethlehem (Matthew 2:13–15). Joseph obeyed the angel's later commands to return to Israel (Matthew 2:19–20) and settle in Nazareth with Mary and Jesus (Matthew 2:22–23). How often does our pride and willfulness get in the way of our obedience to God?

2. St. Joseph was *selfless.* In the limited knowledge we have about Joseph, we see a man who only thought of serving Mary and Jesus, never himself. What many may see as sacrifices on his part, were actually acts of selfless love. His devotion to his family is a model for fathers today who may be allowing disordered attachments to the things of this world distort their focus and hinder their vocations.
3. St. Joseph led by *example.* None of his words are written in Scripture, but we can clearly see by his actions that he was a just, loving, and faithful man. We often think that we primarily influence others by what we say, when so often we are watched for our actions. Every recorded decision and action made by this great saint is the standard for men to follow today.
4. St. Joseph was a *worker.* He was a simple craftsman who served his neighbors through his handiwork. He taught his foster son Jesus the value of hard work. It is likely that the humility Joseph exhibited in recorded Scripture spilled over into the simple approach he took to his work and provided for the Holy Family. We can all learn a great lesson from St. Joseph, patron saint of workers, on the value of our daily work and how it should exist to glorify God, support our families, and contribute to society.
5. St. Joseph was a *leader.* But not in the way we may view leadership today. He led as a loving husband

> when he improvised to find a stable for Mary to give birth to Jesus, after being turned away from the Bethlehem inn. He led as a man of faith when he obeyed God in all things, took his pregnant wife Mary into his home, and later brought the Holy Family safely to Egypt. He led as the family provider by working long hours in his workshop to make sure they had enough to eat and a roof over their heads. He led as a teacher by teaching Jesus his trade and how to live and work as a man.

Looking for additional insight, I sought out two men who have long inspired other men by their example: Matthew Warner and Ken Davison. My first interview is with Matthew Warner, the founder of Flocknote.com, a blessed husband and a grateful father trying his best to balance it all. He's also a prolific blogger, a contributor to the book, *The Church and New Media*, and author of TheRadicalLife.org. Matthew has a BS in electrical engineering from Texas A&M and an MBA in entrepreneurship. He and his family hang their hats in Texas. I was specifically interested in Matthew's views on courage and the role of St. Joseph in the lives of Catholic men.

Matthew, do you think Catholic men struggle to be courageous in today's world? If so, why?

> "Yes. I think it's at least partly because we've forgotten what it means to be a man, which starts with understanding that we are children of God and grows to include the unique responsibilities and job we have as men—sons, brothers, husbands and fathers. When you go down this path, you start to tap into not just

a responsibility to be courageous, but a desire to be so. A need to be courageous. We learn that living a courageous life is one part of what it means to live fully alive—particularly as men."

What are the underlying causes of the issues you have addressed?

"One thing for me has been the need to slow down. To quiet our worldly ambitions (though they are often very good) at times. To pray. To spend time in silence. To examine what it means to be alive, to be sons of God. To really understand who we are, why we're here, and what we are to do. It's about having the right perspective. And when we get too caught up in just being a cog in the world's wheel, our career path, what's next, and so on, we can go through our whole life and never take that time to answer those more important questions. Any good leader knows you first need to identify the goal if you're ever going to reach it."

Have you faced challenges in your own life where courage was required? Will you share what you have learned?

"One particular point was when I chose to leave my secure engineering job and start my own company, flocknote.com. It was truly a matter of following God's plan and being open to something that wasn't necessarily comfortable. But in the end it was exciting and adventurous and creative in the truest sense. It helped me discover who I was and what I was made to do. We were made for courage, not comfort."

Do you think we lack role models? What can we learn from St. Joseph on how we should live as Catholic men?

> "I think there are lots of great role models all around us. The trouble is that instead of surrounding our kids with saints, we surround them with celebrities. So they naturally adopt the wrong role models."

If you could speak with your sons and future grandsons just one more time before your death, what parting words would you share?

> "You are loved. I love you. God loves you. Don't forget who you are, who made you, and what you were made to do."

My second interview is with Ken Davison, cofounder with his wife Kerri of Holy Heroes (a series of CDs in which the lives of saints are dramatized). A former brand manager at Procter and Gamble, he gave up a full-time senior administration position at Belmont Abbey College in North Carolina a few years ago to devote more time to his rapidly growing Holy Heroes business.

He and his wife Kerri have been married for twenty-three years and have eight homeschooled "Holy Heroes" of their own: Virginia, Clara, Margaret, Ken III, Anna, Therese, Lillian, and Caroline.

Ken, you and I have had numerous conversations about the need for courage in Catholic men. Courage always reminds me of St. Joseph and the example he sets for all Catholic fathers and husbands in how we should conduct ourselves. How can Catholic men today embrace St. Joseph's example in a practical way?

"There are many ways to emulate St. Joseph that just jump out at you when you compare his life to ours: making prayer a priority (and trying to really listen to God instead of listing demands), putting care for your wife ahead of having her for your sexual desires, working hard to provide for your family, and trusting in God's providence even when things seem to be tough (at least you haven't had to escape murdering soldiers in the middle of the night to go to Egypt).

"But here's one that is often overlooked. Be obedient to the Church, energetically and scrupulously obedient. St. Joseph was an obedient Jew, following the rules of his faith even when he could have made excuses that they didn't apply to him and his family. Why go to the synagogue to worship when God was living with him? Why go up to Jerusalem for the purification ceremonies for your wife when she didn't need them as both of you knew? Why offer Jesus, the firstborn, to God in the temple and make the sacrifice of the poor of two turtledoves or young pigeons? In fact, note that Joseph often went *beyond* what was required, as he did when he went to the temple for the Presentation of Jesus—it was not required to go to the temple. How many times do we convince ourselves to make a shortcut, to do the minimum where the Church is concerned? The indications are that St. Joseph did quite the opposite. Imitate him by taking your children to Confession. As the father, take the lead in getting them to Mass on time, leading the prayers, and so on. Learn what the Church requires—and then teach it to your children and your wife by word and deed.

"One other thought. Joseph was the head of his family, despite having God and the sinless Mother of God as the only other persons in his household. To whom did the angel appear to tell St. Joseph to take Mary into his home? Gabriel had quite a conversation at the Annunciation and could have easily provided instructions for the Blessed Virgin Mary to pass along to St. Joseph. To whom did the angel appear to tell the Holy Family to escape immediately or Herod's soldiers would take Jesus' life? To whom did the angel appear to tell when to return from Egypt and where to settle in Israel? Each time, God the Father could have sent His messenger to the spouse of the Holy Spirit or to the Second Person of the Holy Trinity, but instead He directed the family through its head, the father. Step up to your task and don't be afraid of the authority God has given you. It is not an honorary or figurehead position—it is a very real authority."

One of the themes of this book is the pressure and negative influence of the secular materialistic culture on Catholic men. How do we live in the world but not be of the world, and keep our sights set on heaven for us and our families?

"Let me build here on what Venerable Fulton Sheen once said. 'If you do not live like you believe, you will begin to believe as you live.' This is a moral universe, and we are here to choose the moral path at every decision point. God made us to live with Him in heaven, and we get there through the life He has made personally for us, in every moment we encounter, in every person we meet, in every decision we make. All that we will take to heaven with us is the love we have here on earth. Nothing else. So, we need to act like it in order to believe it, and by acting on it we learn more and more to believe it. It is really rather simple. Love, true love, is what we *do*, not what we feel—it's not a sentiment, not romance, but action in self-giving, just like Jesus on the Cross.

"God gives us everything we need to get to heaven in every moment, so we simply need to honestly try to do what God wants for us in every circumstance—and for men that is being ready to give up ourselves, our desires, our pleasures, our distractions and pastimes, our well-being, even our lives, for the wife and children and others He has placed around us. If it doesn't help us get them to heaven, then it's not worth it.

"No matter how tired you are, how much you want to blow off steam, how angry you are, how trivial it seems, just run everything through this decision filter. If it doesn't help you get to heaven, then don't do it."

Ken, one last question. If you could speak to a large gathering of Catholic fathers, grandfathers, and aspiring fathers, what would you say to encourage them?

"One word: *gratitude!* God loves you so much that He created you out of nothing. He gave you the gift of life, and then put you on earth so that you could live a life here that gets you eternal life in heaven.

Again and again you'll be selfish and mistaken and willful and try to throw away that gift of eternal life. But God thought of that (thank, God!) and sent His Son to open up heaven for you and to give you the sacraments you need to try, try again. Take advantage of all those sacramental gifts and take advantage of all those moments you have on earth to love through the sacrifice of your own selfish desires.

"And God gave you all sorts of other gifts, too, in the form of people that He wanted to be on earth while you were: your parents to your wife, your children, and all the people you meet. They are all gifts from God to get you to heaven. And the time and place in which you are now and have been and will be are all gifts to help you grow in faith, hope, and love, to equip you for heaven.

"Then He selected an angel to guard and protect you during your whole life. St. Joseph listened to his angel, so you need to ask yours to help you and listen too. Sometimes the people around us may tempt us to go astray, but your guardian angel never will—so ask for help!

"And, wonder of wonders, God even made you into a gift for others. You are a gift to your wife and children, to help them get to heaven. I tell my children when they are upset with me, 'Well, God made me especially for you, and you especially for me, so you've got nowhere to go!' For a Catholic man, being this gift is wondrous and awe-inspiring, because you will get to witness the

> trust placed in you as father and husband that God breathes into your wife when you marry her and into your children when He creates their immortal souls—an all-encompassing trust that only a woman and a child can offer, a trust that is both the gift they join with God to offer to you and the gift He empowers you to offer back to them, through His grace."

As a Catholic father and husband, I will share again that I struggle with the same challenges as many of you and I don't pretend to have all of the answers. I do know that it is not too late to turn away from the things of this world and place our relationships with God, our wives, and our children on a proper footing. Let's ask ourselves right now: Are we prepared to do what is necessary? Are we committed?

As Catholic men, we have a responsibility to be strong fathers and husbands, leaders in our parishes, good stewards in the community, and humble followers of Christ. Let's look to the inspiring example of St. Joseph, patron saint of fathers, workers, and the universal Church for his obedience, humility, selflessness, courage, and the love he showed to Mary and Jesus. If we can emulate St. Joseph even a little each day, we will be that much closer to becoming the men we are called to be.

QUESTIONS FOR REFLECTION

1. Can I recognize in the quiet, yet powerful example of St. Joseph the model I need to follow? Am I willing to make the changes needed?
2. When it comes to my marriage and children, am I selfless? Do I put aside what I may desire for their

greater good? Am I willing to make sacrifices for my family?

3. Matthew Warner made the clear point that men have forgotten how to actually be men. Once we realize this and start down the path of change, we will tap into not only a responsibility to be courageous, but a desire to be so. Am I at this place in my life? Do I desire to be a courageous leader and defender of my family?
4. Ken Davison offered a profound and challenging point. "No matter how tired you are, how much you want to blow off steam, how angry you are, how trivial it seems, just run everything through this decision filter: If it doesn't help you get to heaven, then don't do it." Am I prepared to run my decisions through this kind of filter? Do I see why it is so important?

CHAPTER TEN

On Fathers Instructing Their Children

I was very grateful in that moment to realize
my dad never missed an opportunity to share lessons
that would help me be a better father, husband, and man.
— Author —

I was blessed to grow up with great parents. We didn't have much, but my parents made sure my sister and I had love, discipline, faith, strong values, and an appreciation for the value of hard work. My mother played a vital role in our family, as all mothers do, but I find as I grow older that I am most like my father. I pass many of the lessons he taught me on to my own children and still look to him for wisdom and advice. Look back on your own upbringing. What role did your father play? Were there other role models? Just as many of us live out the lessons we learned in our youth, our children will someday emulate us. They are always watching and we have to decide if we will be their heroic role models who consistently set the right example or relinquish our fatherly responsibilities to a host of bad societal influences. Which will it be?

Our family enjoyed a visit last summer from my then seventy-four-year-old father. These last few years have been difficult for all of us, especially my father, as my mother passed away in 2010 after a long illness. My parents were married for nearly half a century, a rare thing these days. My mother was his best friend, partner and wife, as well as an inspiration to all who knew her.

I recall how we awkwardly spoke of our feelings of loss during his visit and the conversation turned to reflection and a walk down memory lane. Old memories came flooding back for both of us, and I also learned valuable lessons as my dad shared experiences and insights into the multitude of tough decisions he and mom had made over the years. I was very grateful in that moment to realize my dad never missed an opportunity to share lessons that would help me be a better father, husband, and man. That has always been his way. My mother had a similar approach, rooted in a loving style, which I remember fondly.

That conversation and countless others like it over the years with my father has been the catalyst for a lot of introspection about my life and the lives of my children. I know my parents live on in me and their influence often manifests itself in how I behave as a parent, husband, leader, and friend to others. Isn't this the way it plays out for all of us? Don't we hear the reverberating echoes of our parents' and grandparents' lessons in much of what we do and say as adults?

It wasn't always so, as my younger days can attest. I went through typical teen rebellion, thought I knew more than my parents, and felt I could do better than their generation. I was blind to all of the wisdom they had poured into me my entire life. I took for granted the loving and encouraging home they made for our family. The values they taught me seemed old and tired to my teenage ears. I wasn't appreciative of the work ethic they had instilled in me through their own tireless examples. I grew callous to the strong faith they held and walked away from church as a teenager, not to return to any kind of faith until I joined the Catholic Church in 2005 after two long decades in the spiritual wilderness. Through all of this, my parents never stopped praying for me. They never stopped trying to teach me about life and they never ceased to love me. I was blessed to have such a mother and am fortunate to have my father still with us.

I came to my senses in my mid-twenties and the many seeds my parents planted in me began to take root. To paraphrase a famous Mark Twain quote, I was amazed at how smart my parents had become in the years since I had moved away from home! There were numerous stumbling blocks in front of me back then as I was building my career, but I especially remember my father's words of wisdom: "Do the right thing," "Work hard and let your results speak for themselves," "Treat others the way you want to be treated," "Put others before yourself." My mother was a loving and faith-filled woman who shared much in a simple smile or a warm hug while my father was the "teacher" in our home and I find myself sharing these bits of Dad's wisdom with my own children. I am grateful for the solid foundation my parents, especially my father, laid for me when I was growing up.

Do you ever stop and reflect on the lessons you learned in your childhood? Do you share those lessons with your children? There is a desperate need today for a return to the values of past generations and for fathers willing to teach them. The "anything goes" mindset so pervasive in our culture today could benefit from clearer boundaries. Our children would only prosper if they could actually be children for a while and not forced to become shopping crazed consumers addicted to technology at increasingly younger ages. Teaching our kids about faith, values, morality, manners, and the importance of a good work ethic is a critical responsibility for parents today. What if we detach our kids from their electronic pacifiers and force them to play outside? I grew up with a bike, books, and a good imagination. Playing outside and reading were my principal pursuits as a kid and yet, somehow I survived. Harken back to what I hope will be positive memories of the lessons you learned from your parents and grandparents. Don't we have a responsibility to pass along all that is noble and worthwhile to our children?

TWELVE PRACTICAL LESSONS TO TEACH OUR CHILDREN

As I was thinking about some helpful advice to offer fathers in this chapter, I decided not to reinvent the wheel. Below is a list of twelve practical suggestions that come from my vivid memories of how my dad passed along important life lessons to me and my sister. Much of what you will read below was for our personal benefit when we were younger, but he also taught us what we should teach our own children as we reached adulthood. I think we could all make a similar list from our collective past and I hope you find this to be useful.

- MODEL the right behaviors, lead by example, and avoid "Do as I say, not as I do!"
- TEACH the importance of faith, values, and the difference between right and wrong.
- ENCOURAGE excellence and independent thinking.
- LISTEN to their thoughts and ideas with patience and no judgment.
- LOVE your children without reservation, but also enough to say *no* when necessary.
- EXPOSE them to God, nature, beauty, art, music, history, and different cultures.
- GIVE them quality time. Make family time the alternative to unhealthy habits.
- INSTILL an appreciation for hard work and how to be responsible with money.
- CREATE boundaries and explain the rules.
- DISCIPLINE is important.
- RESPECT your elders and authority. Be polite, courteous, and helpful to all.
- INSPIRE your children to give back to the community and help others.
- CHALLENGE kids to develop their minds.

You may have a very different list, but these are some of the most impactful lessons my father taught me and ones I am trying to pass along to my children. It is a scary world out there and I see a generation of children not being equipped to succeed in today's culture. If we don't accept full responsibility for raising and teaching our children, then video games, TV, the Internet, and their peers will likely fill the void. That is the ugly reality.

I would like to dive a little deeper into teaching our kids about our Catholic faith. Guys, as you have learned in this book, we are called to be spiritual leaders as well as providers. Don't delegate our children's faith education to PSR (Parish School of Religion) or Catholic schools. Teaching must begin at home and taught by us working with our wives to set the right example. Here are five actions to consider.

- **Prayer.** Make our prayer lives a priority. Pray over all family meals. Pray with our children at bedtime. Go to Eucharistic Adoration as a family. Inspire children by the sight of their father on his knees in earnest prayer. It all starts with prayer.
- **Example, character, and virtue.** Our children will become whatever we raise them to be. Think about the opportunity we have to let our kids grow up seeing our rock solid faith in God, our devotion to the Church, our consistent character, our virtuous behavior, our devotion to family, our stewardship, our strong prayer life, and our focus on doing the right thing. Or, we can relinquish all of this responsibility to the media, celebrities, and their school friends.
- **Our faith journey.** Be the example for their faith journey. Our kids will likely pray, honor and serve Christ, volunteer, tithe generously, observe the sacraments, and be strong in their faith *if* they grow up in a household where Mom and Dad set the right example.

- **Reading and study.** We can't teach them what we don't understand. Read Scripture and portions of the Catechism together as a family. Read great Catholic books and break down the lessons we learn for our children.
- **Teach a passion for the Eucharist.** From an early age, teach them a reverence and love for the Body of Christ. Help them understand the sacred mysteries and to never take holy Mass lightly.

When I was looking for another voice on the concept of passing the faith on to our children, I had to look no further than Deacon Mike Bickerstaff, my friend, cofounder and Editor-in-Chief of Integrated Catholic Life eMagazine (www.integratedcatholiclife.org). Deacon Mike is steeped in our faith and a natural teacher through his writing and extensive ministry work in the Church. I also know the passion he has for teaching the next generation about our Catholic faith and how to live it out fully every day.

Deacon Mike is a deacon for the Archdiocese of Atlanta. He was ordained in February 2006 and is assigned to St. Peter Chanel Catholic Church where he is the director of Adult Education and Evangelization.

He cofounded the successful annual Atlanta Catholic Business Conference and the Chaplain of the Atlanta Chapter of the Woodstock Theological Center's Business Conference. He also cofounded Chaplains to the St. Peter Chanel Business Association and the Marriages Are Covenants Ministry, both of which serve as models for similar parish-based ministries. Deacon Mike and his wife, Cathy, live in Roswell, Georgia.

They have two grown children, two grandchildren, and a third grandchild on the way.

Deacon Mike, when you consider the future of Catholic children today, what are your biggest concerns?

> "Today's children are growing up in a world that is increasingly hostile to religion in general and Christianity in particular. At present the focus seems to be to keep the observance and practice of religious beliefs within the walls of the church building, but in my assessment, the trend is towards the 'demonizing' of all traditional Christian teachings so that one day they will be considered unacceptable anywhere at any time.
>
> "How will children deal with these trends given the lack of foundation they are receiving of the basics of the faith?"

We know that countless Catholic families are not passing on the faith to their children. What is the special role of a Catholic father in passing on the faith?

> "What is truly important? What is the one thing necessary? If fathers consider these questions, we might begin making better decisions. We are on this planet for the purpose of preparing for and attaining eternal communion with God in heaven. This should be our first and highest priority. As fathers and husbands, we have the added responsibility to lead our families to that same end. Fathers should provide leadership by the example of their lives as well as by their verbal teaching."

What is preventing this from being the norm in Catholic homes today? What are the obstacles?

> "I believe that the primary obstacle is erroneous and dangerous priorities resulting from a failure to understand the nature of our vocation and the purpose for which God made us. That is why I asked the two questions above.
>
> "First, dads must be present to their families. A dad that is present is one who at least places a high priority on his family. That is a good start.
>
> "Second, he must more highly value the interior qualities over the learned and natural talents and skills. For example, as great as artistic, athletic, or academic excellence is, other qualities are more important: integrity, honor, fidelity, compassion, dependability, and love of God."

How can a Catholic man get back on track and show real courage as the spiritual leader of his family?

> "First and foremost, the Catholic husband and father must surrender to Christ. He must take care of his own conversion and spiritual growth. He must live a life that is authentic, that match in word and deed, and a life that conforms to God's plan.
>
> "Second, he must become as involved in the spiritual life and development of his children as he is with their sports activities; be as excited by a son's First Holy Communion as he is by his soccer team's championship."

If you had one opportunity to impress upon Catholic fathers and grandfathers the urgent need for their active participation in the spiritual well-being of their families, what would you share with them?

> "I don't think polls, surveys, and studies would reveal to them anything they don't already know inside: that their good example provided to their children from the earliest possible age is going to have a more dramatic impact that anything else.
>
> "Children watch their parents, especially their fathers, and they record what they see. Children are like video recorders, constantly making home movies. As they grow older, they will encounter challenging opportunities, problems, and circumstances. And they will dig deep into their memories and retrieve the home movie that shows them how you dealt with a similar challenge.
>
> "We are our children's primary teachers. Be sure you know what you are teaching.
>
> "It is difficult enough to grow up gaining eternal wisdom and living according to God's love in today's secularized world in which immorality and irreligion are celebrated. It is almost impossible without a father who is Christ to his family."

I want to challenge you to do a few things. Look at your children when they are sleeping tonight and think about how you can prepare them for the real world. Ask yourself if they are on the path to be faith filled, value driven, hardworking, and selfless people in a world that desperately needs these traits. Finally, be hopeful that one day when they have children of their own, they will hear the echoes of your positive influence on their lives and pass that priceless treasure on to their own children.

QUESTIONS FOR REFLECTION

1. Am I intentional about passing along life lessons to my children?
2. Deacon Mike Bickerstaff challenged a father to "become as involved in the spiritual life and development of his children as he is with their sports activities." Am I guilty of not doing this? Did this chapter help me recalibrate my priorities?
3. What were the most powerful life and faith lessons you learned from your parents, especially your father?
4. Deacon Mike Bickerstaff shared, "Fathers should provide leadership by the example of their lives as well as by their verbal teaching." Is this me today? Why or why not? What will I change to live up to this standard?

CHAPTER ELEVEN

The Virtual Family

Have we thrown in the towel
and allowed the wired world in which we live
to raise our children for us? Are we contributing to the
problem through the examples we are setting
for our children?
— Author —

I took my family out to dinner one evening after my younger son's lacrosse practice. As we were catching up on each other's day and making plans for the coming weekend, I noticed a family had been seated at the table next to us. What struck me as odd was that the dad was on his iPhone answering an email, the mom was texting, and their teenage daughter was also texting—all at the same time! This went on for the duration of the meal and I don't think they had more than five minutes of conversation the entire time they were seated. It was almost surreal for me to see three people sharing a meal while absorbed in the worlds of their individual electronic devices. It occurred to me that I was observing a virtual family in action.

The memory of that evening has stuck with me and I have since observed, with far greater interest, kids and parents focused on the little screens in front of them as they walk, eat, and ride in cars. I brought this topic up at a recent lunch with friends who shared that they were having significant challenges with how much their teens were texting and how they would rather communicate via this medium versus having a real conversation.

Is this progress or are we taking a giant leap backward in the development of our children? Have we thrown in the towel and allowed the wired world in which we live to raise our children for us? Are we contributing to the problem through the examples we are setting for our children?

I want to be clear that I am not anti-technology. It could be that I am feeling a little overwhelmed by the very tools and devices which were meant to make our lives easier and more efficient. I struggle with my own iPhone addiction and responding to the avalanche of emails I receive each day. We have a Wii, computers, and iPhones in our home, and we all watch TV. But we also have clear limits. We restrict our kids' computer and TV time, their music choices, and the content they can view. It is a constant struggle for me and my wife to keep an eye on the potential negative influence of technology and media, but the alternative to being vigilant is the painful road to becoming a virtual family. We can't allow that to happen.

How do we fight back? What can parents do? First of all, let's acknowledge the obvious: our children are growing up with multiple and advanced forms of technology that didn't exist when we were kids. Studies show a clear connection between the explosion of ADD / ADHD cases and the addictive nature of complex video and computer games. A national survey by the Kaiser Family Foundation revealed that minority youth (eight to eighteen year olds) devoted an average of 7½ hours a day to entertainment media! Generation Y (those born between ten and thirty years ago) is also having problems with interpersonal communication. They struggle to relate to other human beings outside of texting and computers. For a sobering and informative look at the challenges facing this generation, read Dr. Tim Elmore's wonderful book, *Generation iY: Our Last Chance to Save Their Future*. Also, take a look at his websites: www.growingleaders.com and www.savetheirfuturenow.com

Now, I would like to take you down a different path. It would be easy for us to think, based on what you have read so far, that our children and the culture are largely responsible for the creation of the "virtual family." I am afraid not. My fellow dads, you and I are mostly to blame. The responsibility to set the right example, create appropriate limits, and offer healthier alternatives for our families rests squarely on our shoulders. We have to take ownership of the fact that we are enabling the problem, or it won't get better. We can't live in denial any longer and immediate action is needed.

Unless we plan to move to a remote cabin in the woods, we are going to face the inevitability of our families being constantly exposed to all forms of media and technology at school, work, and home. That is reality. But we have the ability and obligation to enforce a degree of moderation and offer our families more suitable choices. I am simply suggesting that we replace what is harmful with what is beneficial. Here are six positive actions my wife and I are trying very hard to follow in raising our children.

- **Put away the idols.** Every minute devoted to TV, texting, computers, video games, and our smartphones is time not spent in prayer and serving our Creator. We often forget that we are in the world, but not of the world. We are made for heaven and not this place called Earth. Do our daily actions reflect this?
- **Respond to our vocations.** As Catholics, we should know that our vocation as parents is to help our families (and everyone else) get to heaven. This won't happen unless we put Christ first in our lives and certainly in our homes. If our children see us praying, joyfully attending Mass, going to the Sacrament of Reconciliation, and volunteering our time to help others, they are more likely to follow our example. This is the most important influence we can have over our children. Besides, I don't think our families will attain heaven via email or a text message.
- **Read a book.** Make time for reading and encourage our children to open a book, not a web page. Introduce gadget-free, family reading time. If they only see us on our laptops or watching TV, they will likely model that behavior.
- **Talk to each other.** Generation Y struggles with interpersonal communication, perhaps because of addiction to texting or more likely because we don't reinforce this at home. We have to show

genuine interest in our kid's lives and not accept "fine" as the answer to every question. By the way, moms and dads need to talk to each other as well (the kids model what they see!).

- **Family dinner is sacred.** This one is tough, but make a commitment to have dinner together—every night if possible. Even if it is a quick stop at Chick-fil-A on the way to football practice, meals (with devices turned off!) are the perfect time to catch up and stay involved in our children's lives. Don't forget to share your day as well. My kids are very curious about my work day and my sharing becomes a great teaching opportunity about life in the real world.
- **Don't be a couch potato.** It's a beautiful Saturday afternoon, your favorite movie is on, and you are looking forward to a little down time—and you hear the kids playing video games in the basement. Dads deserve a break (we really do!), but we need to get the kids outside for a bike ride, a hike, throwing the football, or a simple walk as often as possible. Anything that engages them physically and provides meaningful interaction with another human being is a better alternative than Minecraft or Super Mario Brothers.

I know what I am advocating is difficult, but most worthwhile endeavors are going to be challenging. Either we change our habits and positively influence the behavior of our children or we sink into the mindless comfort of our wired worlds and leave our children poorly prepared for the future. A big part of this equation is recognizing that our children need us to be their parents and not their friends. We love our sons very much, but we love them enough to set limits and have rules. Respect must go hand in hand with love as we raise our children or they will not be able to function in the real world.

One man who I suspect has a much better handle on technology challenges than me is Matt Swaim. Matt is the producer of the Son Rise Morning Show, which is syndicated through the EWTN Global Catholic Radio Network. He is the author of *The Eucharist and the Rosary* and *Prayer in the Digital Age*. His latest book, *Your College Faith: Own It!* was co-written with his wife, Colleen. He and his family reside in Cincinnati.

Matt, from your perspective, what impact has technology had on Catholic families with regards to prayer and the way they practice their faith?

> "As with anything, there are always going to be positive and negative aspects to the use of technology in families, dependent upon the user's personal tendencies and formation. On the one hand, I've seen families who no longer make eye contact with one another because they're constantly glued to a screen, and on the other hand, I've seen families huddle around an iPad to read the words of Night Prayer together after dinner. St. Paul, writing two millennia ago, set the standard for use of anything consumable in 1 Corinthians 6:12, writing that *All things are lawful for me*, but not everything is beneficial. *All things are lawful for me*, but I will not let myself be dominated by anything."

What can Catholic fathers do to prevent TV, video games, and the Internet from robbing their families of peace and negatively impacting their faith?

"You can't combat a negative with a negative. I honestly think that so many families rely on technology and screen time to occupy themselves because they simply don't have the energy to look for something better to do. Why go to a park, or the zoo, or play a board game, or read to your children, when it's so much easier to just throw on Netflix and zone out? With so many technological distractions at our immediate disposal, it takes effort to create the kind of home environment that encourages activity and personal interaction. It may sound cheesy, but I'm not above making a list of activities, most of them inexpensive or free, that I can do with my family at a moment's notice: things like going to a park, throwing around a football, grocery shopping, or even cooking together. Even if conversations about faith don't come up in those interactive scenarios, it's still an opportunity for me to build relationships and an avenue of communication where my family feels comfortable enough around me to talk about faith when the time comes."

Do you feel we are allowing these technology enablers to serve as "surrogate parents" for our children? A modern version of the babysitter?

"I can't tell you how many times I've been at the grocery store and seen children occupied with tablets or smartphones while their parents pick through the produce aisle, or how many times I've seen slack-jawed kids stare at mind-numbing children's programming while parents are occupied with household tasks. There are times and places when it can be helpful to sit a child down in front of a movie while you get something important done, but it's all too easy in today's culture to turn the parental reins over to a children's program that may or may not be instilling in your children the values you want them to hold.

"I think the biggest problem with appointing the television, smartphone, or tablet as a babysitter is you don't know what kinds of messages your children are getting from their digital babysitter. What may seem elementary to you, an adult with a reasonably formed conscience, may be entirely new moral territory to your child who hears perspective on an important issue for the first time from an animated character while you're not around."

As a Catholic man who is happily married with a young son, what would you say are the benefits of utilizing technology to help us grow in our faith?

"There are so many great ways to use technology to share the faith in our homes. Whether that's dialing up the liturgy of the hours on a smartphone, printing out coloring sheets or activity pages from places like catholicmom.com or catholicheroesofthefaith.com, or even something as simple as videoconferencing with grandparents after dinner. There are seemingly endless opportunities for using these tools for good. In particular, I love being able to show pictures of great Catholic art to my family by doing a rudimentary internet search. I may never make it to Rome or Florence, but I can bring a small taste of them into my home through the Internet."

From your vantage point, knowing our Catholic young people are already firmly attached to everything from the iPhone to the Xbox, are there ways we can use these tools to reach them with positive messages to help them stay in the Church? Particularly our young men?

"There are two important points to make here. First, it is impossible to ignore the rising tide of technology. It's here to stay. Everyone's plugged in and there's almost nothing we can do about it. If we want to preach the gospel and be lights for Christ in the culture, we have to take his light into the places where people are desperate for it. We have to be culturally savvy, technologically astute, ground-breakingly compassionate, and unashamed of the Savior who has redeemed us.

"Second, we have to make sure that in our rush to engage the culture, we don't get sucked into its guiding principles or overly enamored with its methods of transmission. We can have the best gadgets, the coolest websites, and the best market research, and still be what St. Paul calls *a noisy gong or a clanging cymbal.* And I think one of the main reasons we've lost so much ground with the current generation of technology users is because we've been afraid to boldly

> defend our faith using reason and intellect. In an effort to present a bite-sized faith we've effectively insulted the intelligence of a whole generation, which has come to the general conclusion that people of faith aren't really all that smart and that atheists are the ones who trust them enough to tell them the truth about things. We need to live the faith joyfully, intelligently, and in a spirit of engagement if we want people to look up from their smartphones and ask questions about faith that they may not have even realized were weighing on their hearts."

Let me ask you to imagine a time over twenty years from now. The kids are married, engaged in meaningful careers, and having children of their own. They are active in the practice of their Catholic faith, spend quality time with their families, and give their time unselfishly to help others in the community. This is a happy picture and one I hope we all would like to see become a reality. Now for the big questions: Are we doing everything humanly possible to help our children achieve this kind of future? Are we a "virtual family" or a well-balanced family with its priorities in order?

I don't know about you, but my family still has some work to do.

QUESTIONS FOR REFLECTION

1. What example do I set for my family when it comes to technology? Am I often on the computer when at home? Do I often have a smartphone in my hand?

2. Have I been guilty of allowing my family to drift towards the "virtual family" described by the author? Am I willing to reverse the trend?
3. Matt Swaim makes great points about healthy ways to utilize technology to share our faith and interact with our children. Can I pursue his helpful suggestions and not be consumed by my technology "enablers"? Can I strike the right balance?
4. The author suggests the sacredness of family dinner time and simple conversation as ways to combat the negative aspects of technology. Can I at least take these steps in an effort to make progress towards achieving healthy balance at home?

PART III

WORK AND THE PUBLIC SQUARE

CHAPTER TWELVE

The Difference an Hour Can Make

Maybe it was guilt or the prompting of the Holy Spirit, but nothing at that very moment seemed as important as going home to my wife and sons.
— Author —

On the Monday between this past Christmas and New Year's Day, I had to work for part of the day to meet a few clients, tie up loose ends for the year, and do some preparation for the New Year. It was challenging to be pulled away from my family over the holidays, especially with my easily bored sons out of school during the break. I felt guilty, but I needed to be a good steward of my business and financial responsibilities and get some of my work done.

The last meeting of the day was to be a late lunch with a new client prospect that had been scheduled several weeks before. He called me thirty minutes before our appointment to apologize and say he could not make it. Suppressing my mild irritation, we rescheduled our meeting for another day. I found myself with an unexpected extra hour. What to do? Well, I had a pile of paperwork back at my office to be handled. Perhaps I could leave messages for some of my clients or send them emails in an effort to start filling up my meeting calendar after the holidays. Maybe I could find a quiet place and write that new business blog post which had been on my mind for weeks.

I did none of these things and went home instead.

Maybe it was guilt or the prompting of the Holy Spirit, but nothing at that very moment seemed as important as going home to my wife and sons. As I pulled into the driveway, I saw my thirteen-year-old practicing his jump shot with the new basketball he received for Christmas. Without any words being exchanged we took turns shooting baskets for half an hour. We were simply a father and son having fun together and enjoying being with each other.

Then, he broke the silence. "Dad, why did that kid commit suicide?" My son's jarring question was referring to a local high school student who had killed himself some time ago, which our family had discussed over dinner one night right after the tragedy. After talking about the possible reasons why this young man had chosen to end his own life, we talked about how difficult it is for kids today to deal with the enormous pressure schools, peers, society, and even their own families place on them. I think he was relieved to talk about this topic (he said it had been on his mind for days) and seemed reassured after we finished. I was very grateful at that moment to be reassured that my son takes our Catholic faith seriously and understands the wonderful recourse we have to prayer and the intercession of the saints, especially our Blessed Mother, when we face difficulties. I am especially glad that he felt comfortable talking to me about this painful subject rather than tackling it on his own.

Maybe only other fathers will understand, but I was even more grateful to be there for my son at that moment when he needed to get something off his chest and hear guidance and an explanation from someone he trusted. I would have missed this wonderful opportunity if I had opted for one of the various non-critical tasks I could have chosen instead. There is a profound lesson here that really hit home for me and possibly many of the readers of this post: *we need to be more mindful of the choices we make about where we spend our time.*

As we consider where we spend our time, I encourage all of us to put more thinking and discernment into our busy schedules and recognize that we may need to reset our priorities. Are we letting the unimportant crowd out the important? Are we missing opportunities like the one I was blessed to have with my son because of paperwork, catching up on emails, or returning one more phone call? Do we control our calendars or do our calendars control us? Do we have a disproportionate focus on the pursuit of worldly treasure when we could be spending more time in prayer, at Mass, with our loved ones, or in the service of others in need?

One way to be more thoughtful and discerning about time and priorities is to pray the Daily Examen (see appendix three), which I have used since 2007. In the Examen, we are challenged five times a day to pull away from the world for just a few minutes to pray and reflect on where we are and what we are doing—and discern the lessons God might have for us in the people and situations we encounter throughout the day.

This excellent tool has been a mainstay in my prayer life and I hope every reader of this book will consider using it.

Just a few days ago in a conversation with my son, I witnessed for myself in a simple choice I made the incredible difference an hour can make. As we look forward to another year, what difference will our choices about how we spend our time have on our relationships with Christ, the practice of our faith, the time we spend with our loved ones, and the important causes in need of our assistance? Remember that one of the most meaningful gifts we can give to our children doesn't require fancy wrapping and a big red bow. This gift is simply called *time*.

Over the years I have been blessed to speak with countless Catholic men who are making a positive difference in the lives of other Catholic men. One such man is Andy Mangione. Andy is married to Amy and they reside in Louisville, Kentucky with their two sons, Andrew and Daniel. Andy is active in his parish as a lector and in the Parish Religious Education Program as an instructor. He also hosts a weekly radio program that focuses on fathers raising their sons to be men of God. The program, 'His Father's Apprentice,' is broadcast on Louisville's Catholic radio station, WLCR AM 1040. In his professional life, Andy is vice president of Government Relations for the Association of Mature American Citizens (AMAC).

When he's not working, Andy enjoys spending time with his family, especially driving his sons to car shows in his classic convertible.

I have had the opportunity to discuss this idea of family quality time on several occasions on his radio show, and reached out to him to capture his thoughts for the book.

Andy, you have been involved in Catholic ministry for men for years. What would you say are the biggest challenges facing Catholic men of all ages today when it comes to doing what's important and spending quality time with our loved ones?

> "I would say the biggest challenge facing many Catholic men today is the volume of distractions we face on a daily basis. There are constantly more demands on our time and we surrender our control of our own schedules to secular occasions. What we're doing is sacrificing precious time that could be spent joyfully and faithfully with family for something that takes us away from the home, which is the domestic Church. Organized events can teach wonderful lessons, however, I know of a fellow parishioner whose daughter has attended a big lacrosse tournament that's held every year in a different part of the country over the Thanksgiving Day holiday. They actually play on Thanksgiving Day. Is this really necessary?"

Do Catholic men lack good role models? Where can we see the right example to follow regarding priorities?

> "There are plenty of good Catholic role models for men and many of them are found within your own parish. But you have to make the effort to seek them out. This can be accomplished by simply attending men's fellowship gatherings at your parish. There are more than a few great role models at my fellowship group, men who walk the talk regarding their faith. These are men that I want to be like, and they can be found at every parish if you look for them."

Andy, let me switch gears on you. If you could address a group of Catholic men ranging from teenagers to grandfathers, what would be your counsel to them about living faithful and courageous Catholic lives?

> "I would encourage Catholic men not to be afraid of being Catholic. Practice your faith joyfully. Whether it's making the Sign of the Cross as you pray for a safe trip onboard an airplane for a business trip, or saying a family blessing before a meal in a restaurant, be seen being Catholic. Do something that you don't ordinarily do. Make a retreat with other men, pray with other Catholic groups outside an abortion clinic, talk with your friends and family about your faith, or make the time to pray the Rosary or at least part of it frequently. Challenge yourself to learn more about this wonderful gift of faith that we have as Catholics. I guarantee that the more you learn about the Catholic faith, the more on fire with it you'll be. And guys, be the spiritual leader in your homes, model the faith for your children, and spend time with them!"

In the absence of a father's time with his family you can bet there are countless bad influences ready to take his place and guide his children in the wrong direction. I paraphrase Scott Hahn who once said that in our modern age the father or mother who is willing to walk out of the office after forty hours in order to have more time with their family is the real hero.

Our vocation as husbands and fathers is to help our families get to heaven. Let's slow down enough to set a good example, be present and give them the quality time they need, which in turn is a blessing right back to us.

QUESTIONS FOR REFLECTION

1. Does the author's description of choosing between unimportant emails or other work versus capturing quality moments with our children resonate with me? Have I had a similar experience?
2. When my wife or children need me in those important life moments and I am distracted or busy with something else, where do they turn? Am I abdicating one of my biggest responsibilities when I focus on unimportant tasks instead of being with them?
3. Can I see the connection between actively embracing my faith and having the right priorities? Do I realize that they are connected and if I am living an authentic Catholic faith I will have my priorities in order?
4. The author asked: "Do we control our calendars or do our calendars control us?" What is my response to this question? Do I like the answer?

CHAPTER THIRTEEN

Are We Working for God's Glory or Our Glory?

How often do we get wrapped up in our 'busyness' and convince ourselves it is all for God or our families when possibly we are doing it for ourselves and for our own self-satisfaction?

— Author —

Work should not take up so much of our day that it occupies the time that should be dedicated to God, to our family, to our friends. . . . If this should happen it would be a clear sign that we are not sanctifying ourselves through our work, but rather that we are simply seeking self-satisfaction in it.

— Francis Fernandez —

I am blessed to be a Eucharistic guardian at my parish and one hour each week in the True Presence of Christ has been an incredible blessing in my life, and the reflection and prayer time has been the inspiration for much of my writing. I remember going to Eucharistic Adoration a few years ago with a sincere desire to be still and listen. I usually have too many distractions in my life and I wanted to offer up my burdens in prayer to our Lord, ask for help, and patiently listen for His response. My mind remained calm for only a brief period of time before the usual group of shrill voices in my head began to sound off with, "Why hasn't God answered my prayers yet? I wonder if my client meeting this afternoon will go well. I have a million errands to run after work. I will never get all those emails answered!" And, "I wonder what's for dinner?" I was in the chapel for only a few minutes and I was in deep trouble!

Instead of throwing in the towel, I decided to reflect on my actions and examine where I was getting tripped up. I replayed the events of the previous weeks in my mind. Instead of enjoying the quiet prayer time I so dearly love early each morning, I was filling that period with work on the Integrated Catholic Life eMagazine, writing blog posts and articles for various outlets, and answering emails. As I examined the highly caffeinated and frantic pace I had been keeping I realized I was acting like the workaholic that I thought I had rid myself of years ago when I converted to the Catholic Church. The Jesuit Daily Examen (see appendix three) that provided me brief moments of prayer and reflection throughout my busy day had been crowded out by my busy schedule. I was jumping into work issues during the last hour of the day when my wife and I usually enjoy some quiet time together. I felt like I was out of control and desperately needed to get back on track.

Prayer was not working, and reflecting on my recent frantic schedule was depressing, so I decided to focus on my spiritual reading for help. I have always found great comfort and sage wisdom over the years in the writings of Francis Fernandez and his wonderful series of books *In Conversation with God*. I turned to the appropriate page (259) for that day in Volume 3, which is about the dignity of work. I had an epiphany a few minutes later as I read the following words I so desperately needed: "Work should not take up so much of our day that it occupies the time that should be dedicated to God, to the family, to our friends. . . . If this should happen it would be a clear sign that we are not sanctifying ourselves through our work, but rather we are simply seeking self-satisfaction in it." I had fallen into the trap of thinking that all of my hard work in my professional life and for the Church was always for other people, when perhaps one of my motivations had been for my own self-satisfaction. It was very difficult to admit, but I had to admit it might be true.

From the gift of self-awareness Christ gave me in reflecting on my recent behaviors to the realization that I need to make some changes, and the epiphany He revealed to me in the writings of Francis Fernandez, Christ absolutely answered my prayer that morning. Our Lord gave me everything He knew I needed. I realized I would have some hard work and a lot of prayer in front of me to make the necessary changes, but I needed to restore peace and a sense of balance to my life.

A few days later, I heard a homily from our parish's former parochial vicar, Father Henry. He spoke about getting rid of the obstacles between us and Christ during Lent (as we discussed in chapter one). Father Henry challenged us to examine what was getting in the way of a stronger relationship with Christ and to give up those harmful obstacles during Lent. I had another epiphany as I realized I desperately needed more quiet time. I would never have peace and a return to the rich prayer life I once enjoyed unless I eliminated most of my distractions. So, I gave up TV, radio, and unnecessary computer time during that Lent, and have worked hard at minimizing these distractions as much as possible since that time. The change has had an enormously positive impact on my life!

Before you decide I'm crazy and this is not practical, indulge me for a little while longer. I am in my car more than ninety minutes each day. Eliminating most TV time has helped me reconnect to my spiritual reading in the evening. I have eliminated unnecessary computer time outside of my work and Integrated Catholic Life eMagazine editing responsibilities, and I have carved out more meaningful time with my family. By turning off the radio and enjoying the silence, or listening to Gregorian Chant and other beautiful music, I have turned what was once unproductive time into wonderful prayer and reflection time. These efforts are helping me get back on track and I pray daily that I will keep my focus on the lessons I have learned.

So, my brothers, what have I learned from these experiences? All of my hard work is absolutely meaningless if it is not given up for God's greater glory instead of my own personal satisfaction. I need to be careful about scheduling every minute of my life. The buzz surrounding our busy lives is not likely to be going away, but our reactions can improve our sense of peace and our relationships with Christ. If we make consistent and intentional efforts to unplug from the noise and reconnect with God in prayer and silence, that may perhaps be one of the best uses of the scarce time we have each day. My pride, as usual, got in the way, but this experience taught me once again valuable lessons in humility. This experience reconfirmed one of the central themes of this book: *I know I am made for heaven and not this world.* I will likely always be fumbling and stumbling towards that heavenly home, but at least I am on the correct path and moving ahead.

As I have done throughout *Journey to Heaven*, I sought candid input from another voice who could credibly speak on this subject. That person is Kevin Lowry. Kevin M. Lowry is an enthusiastic convert to the Catholic faith who spent over twenty years in secular financial and executive management roles. Kevin currently serves as Chief Operating Officer for The Coming Home Network International, a Catholic apostolate that assists non-Catholic clergy and laity on the journey to the Catholic Church and beyond. He is also chief financial officer for RevLocal, a rapidly growing internet marketing company.

Kevin's first book is entitled *Faith at Work: Finding Purpose Beyond the Paycheck*. The book encourages readers to integrate their faith and work in order to discover a new sense of purpose and draw closer to Christ. He has also written for numerous Catholic publications and websites such as *Envoy, The Catholic Answer, New Covenant, The Integrated Catholic Life*, Catholic News Agency, and Catholic Exchange. His website and blog are at www.gratefulconvert.com. Kevin and his wife Kathi have eight children.

Kevin, in your experiences as a business leader and writer, what do you think are the main challenges for Catholic men in the workplace today?

> "One of the biggest challenges is being lured into a sense that what we see is all there is. It's easy to become

focused on worldly values and compartmentalize our faith. Particularly in the context of today's highly competitive workplace environment, there are constant pressures to do more with less, be great leaders, grow in responsibility, make more money—and do it all while maintaining balance at home. This can lead to a set of externally imposed expectations that can be overwhelming.

"At the same time, the biggest problem tends to exist between our ears. In my view, the single biggest challenge for Catholic men in the workplace is to maintain a sincere attitude of humility. This is becoming an increasingly rare characteristic, although thankfully Pope Francis has been leading by example in this area. In so many ways humility is a foundational virtue and the basis of true teamwork. It's therefore not only our biggest challenge but our greatest opportunity.

"From a practical standpoint, there's also a natural tendency for men in particular to become focused on work to the exclusion of other important aspects of life. There are invitations to disorder all around us, clamoring for our attention. As a result, growing in holiness is made all the more urgent."

Why do Catholic men struggle with these issues? How do they overcome them?

"Catholic men need to make a living just like everyone else. So we go find a job somewhere, and it's really easy to get sucked into the culture of whatever organization or environment we find ourselves working within. We want to be good at our job, and we want to succeed, but there may be areas of conflict with our faith—if a company is completely focused on making money, for example.

"Now, this may sound like capitalist heresy but think of it this way. If you're a professional basketball team, you want to win the game. Do you win by constantly watching the scoreboard? No. You play the game to the best of your ability and the scoreboard reflects your efforts. Money is a means, not an end. The proper end is people. Serving people *is* serving God. Making money is great, but it can't be the sole reason for the existence of a company or a person.

"I used to work in a service oriented CPA firm. If I would have approached prospective clients stating that my goal was to make money, what would they have thought? Instead, the focus was on service, delivering value for their money. This resonated. With for-profit, non-profit, governmental organizations, it doesn't matter—the primary goal should be service.

"As men, we often fall into the trap of self-identifying who we are with what we do for a living. I've been guilty of this too. It takes a spiritual perspective to break free. Our egos tell us it's all about us, but that's not what our faith says. If we really get this right, and humility replaces pride as a habitual way of thinking, there's no limit to what God can accomplish through us."

You mentioned pride and how often our lack of humility gets in the way. Do you feel that we, as Catholic men, often forget we should work for His Glory instead of our own?

> "Oh, no question! This is why it's so important to allow the faith to permeate every aspect of our lives: work, money, relationships, you name it. That's why I'm very grateful to have suffered major failures in my life in addition to wonderful successes (the opening line of my conversion story is 'One of the best things that ever happened to me spiritually was getting kicked out of Franciscan University of Steubenville'). It seems counterintuitive, but really screwing up every now and again helps us to maintain utter dependence upon God.
>
> "In the end, part of the perspective we require flows from grace, and as Catholics, one of the most extraordinary aspects of our lives is sacramental grace. I still shake my head in amazement over being able to receive the Eucharist. As a convert, I think Confession is one of the most powerful experiences ever. And for us married guys, the Sacrament of Marriage is among the most underappreciated sacraments around. My wife really does have a heavily sanctifying effect on me, in a good way, and also provides impediments to my pride.
>
> "Just to illustrate the point a bit further, I've enjoyed a pretty successful career thus far, despite having a wife and eight kids. But is it really despite the family, or is it because of them? With the benefit of hindsight,

I now believe that they have been the reason for my success in ways I never considered earlier. I always worked harder, was more focused, took greater risks, and attempted to be more effective precisely because they were relying on me. I didn't succeed in spite of them, it was *because* of them and *for* them. It's a beautiful thing."

You and I have both written extensively about integrating faith and work. Don't we, as Catholic men, have a special calling to live out our faith at work? Is this happening?

"One of the reasons I wrote my book *Faith at Work: Finding Purpose Beyond the Paycheck* was that I wanted to encourage people to integrate faith and work in simple, practical ways. It's almost like we're conditioned to think of the faith as a downer, a fun-sucker, or a rigid way of thinking, and nothing could be further from the truth. When we apply our faith to any area of life, we bring the wisdom of the ages and the grace of our Creator to bear. If we live our faith in our work, Catholics become better workers and workers become better Catholics.

"Let's face it, we have a calling to live our faith at work and everywhere else. By bringing our masculine virtues to bear, there is a huge opportunity, and it happens, one person, one day at a time. It can happen in the little things, like saying a quick prayer before a difficult meeting or discussion, honoring women by treating them as we would have other men treat our wives or daughters, or handling challenges with courage and a sense of hope. The effect transcends our own efforts, since the Holy Spirit can use even our imperfect actions and penetrate human hearts."

What practical advice do you have for Catholic men from recent college graduates to grandfathers near retirement age regarding how they should view their work and careers?

"I would encourage them, first and foremost, to be men of prayer. I know some guys, otherwise good Catholics, who think that there's something wrong with praying about their work. That's crazy! God wants us to be in relationship with Him, and part of that relationship is praying about our day, every day, work included. I like to begin every day with a Morning Offering, a simple prayer offering all the events of our upcoming day to the Lord, and asking for him to sanctify our efforts. He's with us regardless of how things go.

"In addition, it's important to recognize that our work is a fundamental aspect of our growth in holiness. In a certain sense, the workplace is the ideal environment to grow in virtue. I recall having a tyrant for a boss early in my career. It wasn't much fun at the time, but in retrospect it was a formative process, since I learned what type of manager I *didn't* want to become. It helped me learn, at a visceral level, to treat people with dignity in the workplace. So even the difficult situations we encounter can be huge advantages from a spiritual standpoint.

> "Finally, I would encourage them to use the opportunity our work presents us to love others with the agape love Christ demonstrated so beautifully for us. The workplace is full of hurting people, and that love is not only our hope, it's theirs too.
>
> "May the Lord bless your faithful work!"

How often do we get wrapped up in our "busyness" and convince ourselves it is all for God or our families, when possibly we are doing it for ourselves and for our own self-satisfaction? Hard work and enjoying that work is not the issue. Allowing that work and busy activity to come between us and Christ, the authentic practice of our Catholic faith and time with our loved ones is the issue, and I have encountered countless men who have admitted they share this problem. Let's consider the experiences I have shared in this chapter and the wise counsel offered by Kevin Lowry to reflect on our own lives. Where have we gotten off track? Pray in earnest for peace, wisdom, and the courage to put work in the proper place, and remember to perform that work for God's greater glory and not our own. Never hesitate to seek out the intercession of St. Joseph, patron saint of workers, fathers, and the Catholic Church.

St. Joseph, please pray for me and all Catholic men
facing similar challenges that we will have the courage
to overcome our pride and weakness
to focus on eliminating those things which separate us
from Jesus, our families, and our final destination in heaven.

QUESTIONS FOR REFLECTION

1. As I consider what the author and Kevin Lowry have shared, have I allowed my work to negatively impact my prayer life, relationship with Christ, and the amount of quality time I spend with my family?
2. One of the themes of this chapter we can infer is that we can work for worldly success or we can work to attain heaven. Are the two mutually exclusive? Can I be successful and provide for my family while still putting Christ first and allowing time for my faith and family?
3. Ponder Kevin Lowry's words: "As men, we often fall into the trap of self-identifying who we are with what we do for a living. I've been guilty of this too. It takes a spiritual perspective to break free. Our egos tell us it's all about us, but that's not what our faith says." Am I guilty of having my identity completely wrapped up in my career?
4. Am I prepared to follow the author's prescriptions for finding peace and prayer time to reduce the noise in my life? What will I commit to do starting right now? Who will hold me accountable?

CHAPTER FOURTEEN

Integrating Faith and Work

In the practice of our Catholic faith, we are faced with a choice between a compartmentalized life or an integrated life where faith, family, and work are unified and centered in Christ.

— Author —

In the last chapter we examined our tendency to let work and "busyness" crowd out our prayer time, family time, pursuit of heaven, and responses to this common challenge. Now let's come at work in a different way: How do we integrate our faith with our work? If you think about it, most of us will likely spend the majority of our adult (awake) lives in the workplace. A typical eight-hour work day accounts for a third of the total day, with the other two-thirds devoted to sleeping, family, friends, faith, and so on. In the practice of our faith, do we consider the workplace as an opportunity to be open about our

Catholic beliefs or do we ignore this vital time and only think about being Catholic the other sixteen hours a day?

I suspect many of us will agree that the workplace today is perceived as a challenging environment to be open about our Christian beliefs. Political correctness and rigid company policies have led many of us to compartmentalize our faith in an unhealthy and unnatural way. I often hear men say, "I just leave my faith at the door when I get to work." But how can we possibly separate our spiritual selves from our physical being?

In *Gaudium et spes*, the Second Vatican Council weighed in with this declaration: "This split between the faith which many profess and their daily lives deserves to be counted among the more serious errors of our age. . . . The Christian who neglects his temporal duties, neglects his duties toward his neighbor and even God, and jeopardizes his eternal salvation. Christians should rather rejoice that, following the example of Christ Who worked as an artisan, they are free to give proper exercise to all their earthly activities and to their humane, domestic, professional, social and technical enterprises by gathering them into one vital synthesis with religious values, under whose supreme direction all things are harmonized unto God's glory" (no. 43).

How can we overcome secular obstacles to our faith and fully embrace Christ in every aspect of our day, especially work?

The concept of being Catholic at work is a daunting idea for many and the thought of acting, thinking, and leading through the lens of our faith is an alien concept. In my profession, I encounter scores of business men and women who incorrectly perceive "faith at work" as leading Bible studies in the break room over lunch or loudly evangelizing coworkers. It rarely occurs to us to think about our own faith journeys, the example we set for others, and the Christ inspired joy we should radiate, as the most effective ways to share our faith. Letting others see Jesus Christ at work in us is a powerful form of witness that will attract others who want what we have in our lives.

Ponder the words of St. Pope John Paul II in his Apostolic Exhortation, *Christifideles laici*: "The fundamental objective of the formation of the lay faithful is an ever-clearer discovery of one's vocation and the ever-greater willingness to live it so as to fulfill one's mission" (no. 58). "The lay faithful, in fact, 'are called by God so that they, led by the spirit of the Gospel, might contribute to the sanctification of the world, as from within like leaven, by fulfilling their own particular duties. Thus, especially in this way of life, resplendent in faith, hope and charity they manifest Christ to others.'" (no. 15, citing *Lumen gentium,* no. 31).

The mission of the lay faithful forces us to consider the workplace as fertile ground in which we can do God's work. As we know from numerous Scripture passages and clear Church teaching, we are all called to lead lives of holiness and to be witnesses for Christ. Therefore, our actions in the workplace necessarily become a critical component of responding to that call.

There are numerous obstacles in the way of us achieving the integration of our faith with our work, but in my experience three of them consistently surface: *silos, time,* and *surrender.*

OBSTACLE 1: SILOS

Does the earlier statement, "I just leave my faith at the door when I get to work" resonate with you? Having lived a compartmentalized existence for most of my life, I have learned how to recognize these "silos" in others and it is very common.

Yet, I would suggest that deep down many of us desire a more *integrated life*, a life in which Christ is at the center of our daily thoughts and actions at both work and home. I believe that promoting this integration will help us all become better Christians and reverse the negative effects—moral, emotional, and spiritual—of keeping our faith separate from the rest of our lives.

Overcoming this obstacle will not be simple or easy, but we must follow the guidance I shared earlier from St. Pope John Paul II in *Christifideles laici* and see our daily activities, including our work, as opportunities to join ourselves to God and serve His divine will. We all play multiple roles in life: fathers, husbands, brothers, leaders, employees, students, and so on. But the most important role and responsibility we have is to be faithful Catholics. Being faithful Catholics in *thought, word,* and *deed* at all times will allow us to unify our lives and rise above our natural tendencies towards compartmentalization and silos. I know this is easy to say and possibly difficult to do, but it is necessary nonetheless.

OBSTACLE 2: TIME

Do you have challenges, like me, with having enough time each day? Most days my work calendar is completely filled with meetings and phone calls. Outside of the work day, I am focused on helping my wife get the kids ready for school, family dinner time, evening time with the kids, youth sports, bed time reading and prayers with the kids, time with my wife, infrequent exercise, answering emails I couldn't get to during the day, and then falling asleep exhausted after reading two pages of the book that has been on my nightstand for months! Sound remotely familiar?

Where does our relationship with Christ fit into our busy day? The key here is to recognize that Christ should never compete for our time and that living our busy lives and putting Him first are not mutually exclusive! He is not to be considered an *addition* to our lives. He is the *reason* for our lives. Let's stop viewing the daily practice of our faith as adding more time to already packed schedules and instead focus on integrating our lives with Christ at the center of everything we do.

OBSTACLE 3: SURRENDER

If we refuse to surrender, sincerely giving up control of our lives to Christ, we face an enormous obstacle to living out our faith in the workplace or any other place. I know full well what my life was like before surrendering to Christ in 2005. I said no to Him for over two decades and the effort was exhausting. Now I say yes and that has made an enormous difference in my life. All I had was family and work prior to my conversion and I thought I was in charge of my life and future. I thought I was being the strong husband and father that *my* father had been when I was growing up. I thought I was in charge.

My brothers, I still struggle every day with pride and making sure Christ is first in every aspect of my life. I have the same challenges as most men, but knowing that He will forgive me, love me, and guide me keeps me coming back again and again to the place where I pray the words, "Lord, I surrender. Please lead and I will follow." The key to overcoming the obstacles of silos and time is *surrender.*

You may face different challenges to being Catholic at work, but these obstacles have consistently been issues for me and countless others who I have encountered. The question to answer for ourselves is simple. *What will we do differently to be fully Catholic in the workplace and not leave our faith at the door?*

SIX PRACTICAL IDEAS FOR INTEGRATING OUR CATHOLIC FAITH WITH WORK

I have always been drawn to achievable and actionable ideas and I would like to share these six practical actions for living out our Catholic faith at work, which I am trying to follow.

DEVOTE ONE HOUR OF EACH DAY TO PRAYER AND READING

The time-challenged among us are silently screaming, *no way*! But, I am telling you it is absolutely achievable. Would we ever consider *not* giving our loved ones an hour a day? Doesn't God deserve at least an hour of our time as well? Here are some easy ways to achieve an hour of combined prayer and faith-based reading each day.

- Try getting up fifteen minutes earlier each morning to read Scripture or some other great Catholic book or resource which follows the magisterium of the Catholic Church.
- Pray the Morning Offering before leaving the house each morning.
- Pray the Angelus throughout the day.
- Pray the Rosary or five decades of it on the way to work or during exercise.
- Do the Jesuit Daily Examen mentioned so often in this book. The Examen requires you to stop, reflect, and pray five times a day for just a few minutes.

Put it on your calendar and make it part of your routine.

- Say a blessing over every meal, regardless of our companions.
- Pray with our families at bedtime.
- Pray a family Rosary or five decades of it.
- Read a few pages of Scripture or a Catholic spiritual work before going to sleep.

Let's make good use of the calendars on our smart phones, or whatever calendar works best for you, but prayer and reading will only happen if we make time for them. Consider this thought from Dr. Peter Kreeft: "The first rule for prayer, the most important first step, is not about how to do it, but to just do it; not to perfect and complete it but to begin it. Once the car is moving, it's easy to steer it in the right direction, but it's much harder to start it up when it's stalled. And prayer is stalled in our world" ("Time" from http://www.peterkreeft.com/topics/time.htm).

DEVOTE MORE TIME TO THE EUCHARIST

Do you want to fully experience Christ and be closer to Him during the work day? Know what parishes are on your way to work or near your office. Seek out the True Presence of Christ in the Eucharist in daily Mass when possible, and spend quiet time before the Blessed Sacrament in Eucharistic Adoration every week. Again, Masstimes.org and smartphone app are very helpful in finding the nearest churches for Mass and visits to the Blessed Sacrament. We Catholics have a wonderful gift in the Eucharist and we should seek Him out at every opportunity.

BE A LIGHT FOR CHRIST

What does being a light for Christ mean? How can it be manifested in us? Francis Fernandez shares this observation from *In Conversation with God:* "Jesus said to his disciples: '*You are the light of the world.*' The light of the disciple is the light of the Master himself. In the absence of this light of Christ, society becomes engulfed in the most impenetrable darkness. Christians are to illuminate the environment in which they live and work. *A follower of Christ necessarily gives light.* The very witness of a Christian life, and good works done in a supernatural spirit, are effective in drawing men to the faith and to God. Let us ask ourselves today about our effect on those who live side by side with us, those who have dealings with us for professional or social reasons. Do they see this light which illuminates the way that leads to God? Do these same people feel themselves moved, by their contact with us, to lead better lives?" (Vol. 5, 69–70).

LET LOVE DRIVE OUR ACTIONS

Agape, the Greek word for selfless love, is the magic elixir that should drive our daily work activities. It is by acting in a selfless and charitable way towards others and putting their needs before our own that people will truly begin to see Jesus at work in us. It is so easy to focus on our own desires and needs, but take up the challenge to make today about serving others. Even the little acts of selfless kindness will have a dramatic impact on the people around us.

PRACTICE ACTIVE STEWARDSHIP

Do you and your company give back to the community? 1 Peter 4:10 says, *As each has received a gift, employ it for one another as good stewards of God's varied grace.* Get involved, make a difference, and contribute. Perhaps if we lead, our company will follow. Look for opportunities to reach out to the "Lazarus" in our lives today (from the parable of the rich man and Lazarus in Luke 16:19–31). Lazarus may be a depressed or troubled coworker, a client who is dealing with personal tragedy, or the homeless and hungry outside the walls of our office building. Consider 1 John 3:17: *But if any one has the world's goods and sees his brother in need, yet closes his heart against him, how does God's love abide in him?* Men, please remember that stewardship is more than writing a check or donating online.

START WITH THE END IN MIND

I can't think of a better motivation for practicing our Catholic faith in the workplace than this mental image. Imagine Jesus greeting you in heaven with the words, *Well done, good and faithful servant* (Matthew 25:23). The road to heaven necessarily leads through the workplace. We have a lifetime, including our time at work, to love and serve the Lord. Will we use it wisely? What will Jesus say to us at the end of our lives?

My intent in sharing these actions is to show how simply we can alter our lives in a way that integrates faith and work, and puts us on the path to a Christ-centered, meaningful life. I try every day to do the actions I have shared and I assure you that I struggle like anyone else. Our challenge is to practice them not as a bunch of new "to-dos," but as part of a broader, unifying approach to a balanced and meaningful life that places Christ *first* in all areas of our lives.

In the practice of our Catholic faith, we are faced with a choice between a compartmentalized life or an integrated life where faith, family, and work are unified and centered in Christ. We are asked to "change our hearts," to let go of our attachments to material things and place Him first in our lives. We are asked to let others see Jesus within us and to share our joy with others. Our humble and virtuous example to others throughout the day will positively influence their behavior and individual faith journeys. An active prayer life, one which turns our day into a conversation with God and firmly places His desires before our own, will open us up to receive boundless grace. We have an opportunity, especially in the workplace, to be beacons of light and good examples of Christ's redeeming love.

We can't be two-thirds Catholic. It doesn't work and is counter to our calling. I encourage each of us to reflect on the lessons in this chapter immediately. The world desperately needs it. With the help and guidance of the Holy Spirit we can do it. The time is now.

QUESTIONS FOR REFLECTION

1. Was this chapter an eye opener for me regarding living out my Catholic faith at work?
2. The author identified silos, time, and surrender as three obstacles to integrating faith and work. Do these resonate with me? Do I have others? If so, what are they?
3. The author wrote, "Letting others see Jesus Christ at work in us is a powerful form of witness that will attract others who want what we have in our lives." Does this help me see that faith at work is not necessarily a Bible study or noisily evangelizing

my coworkers, but how I live my faith and express my joy?

4. The author reminds us that "the road to heaven necessarily leads through the workplace." Can I afford to ignore my workplace as another opportunity to live out my faith? What is holding me back?

CHAPTER FIFTEEN

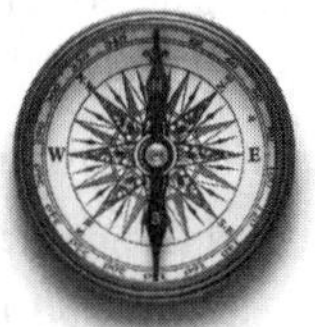

What is Really Important?

We spend so much time trying to manage or stay ahead
of the burdens of the life we have created
that we don't make time for Jesus.
— Author —

We have addressed at various times in this book the importance of having our priorities in the right place. You might wonder why I have devoted an entire chapter to "what is really important" in life. The answer is the overwhelming majority of Catholic men I encounter mention this is an almost insurmountable problem in their lives. They understand the need for priorities and know they need to act, but they are not sure where to go or what to do.

We know the basics: Christ is first, family is second, and work is third. Not only should Christ be first in our lives, but He demands *all* of us—100 percent all the time. In return, He gives us everything we need, *not* necessarily what we want. This means Christ takes precedence over family and certainly our work, but we often get these priorities mixed up. Guys, this idea of surrender that we explored deeply in chapter two is sometimes very difficult for us. We like control and predictability. Many men would argue that there is a complexity and depth to this idea of priorities that is often fueled by different emergencies or imbalances in their lives. The father who loses his job or the husband whose wife has cancer may feel driven to focus on those areas to the detriment of his relationship with Christ. But still, Christ comes first—before our families, our work, our crises, before everything. If we get that straight and follow Him, we will have His love, His strength, and whatever we need to tackle the problems that come our way if it is His will.

I suspect that part of the way to grasp these priorities is to focus on leading simpler lives. We often make life complicated in our illogical pursuit of toys and an inflated lifestyle that does not matter. We spend so much time trying to manage or stay ahead of the burdens of the life we have created that we don't make time for Jesus. We aren't truly following Him when we are focused on worldly matters. *No servant can serve two masters; for either he will hate the one and love the other, or he will be devoted to the one and despise the other. You cannot serve God and mammon* (Luke 16:13).

To really address this idea of what is important, I sought out two hard-working Catholic husbands and fathers I respect who are all too familiar with the pressures of the world and setting the right priorities: Rob Kaiser and Rick Swygman. Pay close attention to the substance these two men offer us.

Rob Kaiser is a lifelong Catholic who married Lynn twenty-two years ago. They have four children ages seventeen to four: Maggie, Mike, Grace, and Clare. Rob is a partner in a marketing research company, Summit Research, where he uses the methodology skills he learned from his PhD in psychology and years in marketing to help clients better understand their customers and develop appropriate strategies. He founded catholicdadsonline.org in 2007 to be a visible presence and outlet for Catholic dads. He serves on the board of Catholics at Work OC and the La Habra Life Center, and is active in his parish.

Rob, I have long appreciated the great work you do in encouraging Catholic men through your excellent catholicdadsonline. org website. As you consider your own life and the lives of the Catholic men you encounter, what should we be focused on in terms of priorities?

> "At one level this is an easy question to answer. We must be men of character, or in more 'Catholic' language, men of virtue. But what does it means to be a man of virtue? We have the cardinal virtues (prudence, justice, fortitude, and temperance) and the theological virtues (faith, hope, and love). But that is a lot and how do we start? What is our hook?
>
> "I once heard a recorded show by Archbishop Fulton Sheen about the different roles of fathers and mothers. He claimed that, among other differences, fathers tended to reflect God's justice and mothers tended to reflect God's mercy. Of course fathers and mothers, men and women, are called to reflect both in their lives (and other aspects of God as well), but there is truth that men are called in a way that is not the same as women, and that idea of 'being 'just' is important

here. The Catechism defines justice as 'the constant and firm will to give their due to God and neighbor' (1807). I think that is the place to start as a man, married or not, father or not. We are called to be 'just men' and to demonstrate justice throughout our lives.

"First and foremost, we are called to give to God that which is due to Him by His very nature. It is right to give to God all of our heart, mind, and strength, to love Him and serve Him before everything else. This must be our top priority. This is the reason He created us—that we might be with Him. He gave us everything we are and have, including His very own life, and He calls us to give all back to Him. This doesn't mean we are all called to live a monastic life, though indeed some men are called to that life. It does mean two things: (1) that we place our relationship with God above all else and that everything else be with and for Him. We must be men of prayer. Our relationship with God is the most important thing in our lives. He is the source and summit of everything; and (2) that God must be a part of everything else we do. Whether it is our marriages, our families, our work, our friendships, or our leisure activities, whatever it is, God needs to be a part of it.

"After giving God His due, we must give to others what is their due. We start to figure what others are 'due' by first considering *who* they are. No matter who they are, I can say two true things about them that have profound implications. First, they are persons made in the image and likeness of God Himself. Second, they are children of God who made them.

All of them are our brothers and sisters in the family of mankind, and many are in a special relationship with us as brothers and sisters in Christ. Our wives, children, parents, friends, and even strangers are reflections of God and are in relationship to us. We are called to treat them in a way fitting that status. When I think about it, it hits me like a ton bricks, both how awesome that is and how often I fail at it (I am definitely still a work in progress).

"Notice that starting with justice, in relation to God and neighbor, we end up talking about what looks a lot like Christian love. We cannot separate the idea of justice and love. Love is what is due. The proper response to God's love is love itself. Too often though, the language of 'love' is difficult for us as men today. At least it can be for me. One of the hard things about being a 'Christian man' today is that too many forces, some of them well intentioned (others more nefarious), twist the concept of a Christian man into something it does not need to be. Some use the language of love to neuter the concept of masculinity. This is unfortunate because it is not true. We can be, indeed must be, strong, courageous Christian men with our own masculine personalities, who love like men love, who protect and defend and create. The love we are called to is not something that rejects our masculinity; it is something that is integral to it.

"On the flip side, other forces want to tell us that being a man means not being Christian. Sex, power, and business are just a few areas proposed as essential to being men and opposed to being Christian. This is half right. These areas are essential to the lives of most men. But this is not antithetical to being Christian. Pornography, abuse of position, and greed are antithetical to being Christian. Being a real man, in just relation to God and others, has a sexuality appropriate to his vocation, is a leader and protector of others, and treats others fairly in business. While popular culture paints a real man as incompatible with Christianity (something akin to an older adolescent), the truth is that we can only be real men when in proper relation to God and man. That is what it is to be a Christian man. A real Christian married man loves and is devoted to his wife. He leads and provides for his family, placing them as a priority in his life. He treats his children as fellow children of God. A real man lays down his life every day for those God has put in his life. Lots of times that looks like prayer, relationships, work, and leisure, but through it all we are connected to God and one another and must always come back to that."

What gets in the way of us pursuing these priorities?

"Too many things get in the way, but I think there are two that stand out. First is our culture. We are in a world that tells us that pride and selfishness are good. Our consumer culture is about satisfying ourselves. Our business culture too often centers on getting ahead at all costs. Deeper than these is the degraded role of being a real man in our society. We are encouraged to be that adolescent free of parental restrictions to do whatever he wants. The role of a father is too often the butt of jokes. We are in a world where pornography is a billion dollar industry and men are addicted to this evil. We are told that it is only business, to leave our ethics at the door. We are supposed to do whatever it takes to get ahead, and then do what it takes to get what we want outside of work. Our culture sets us up to be slaves to greed and our basest pleasures. Because these speak to our pride and selfishness, too often we willingly extend our necks for the iron collar this slavery demands and then think we have it good, except for the meaninglessness of such an existence.

"The other problem is *us*. Let our tendency to pride and selfishness go for now. I think there is a bigger problem. As a group, men are action oriented. We get things done. We solve problems, we accomplish goals, we are on it! This is not a bad thing in its proper place. It is part of how God created us. He is action oriented; just look at what He created! The problem is that our action also tends to be grounded in a do-it-myself I-am-in-charge mentality. We don't want to let go of our control. We use the skills we have to assess, decide, and act as self-sufficiently as possible. Here's the thing: A Christian man needs to start with receptivity before acting. I think this is why spirituality is easier for women. They are more naturally receptive. They listen and ponder and consider more easily than men. Christianity demands that we start with receptivity. Like Mary at the Annunciation, we must be open to God and His will. We first must turn over control, then we go forth and act and do and accomplish.

Being Christian requires us to stop first so that we follow God rather than lead Him. I think that too many of us are not willing to create the time and space when we can be receptive to God in prayer or in reading Scripture. We are so busy doing, we fail to listen and discern."

Do you have any thoughts, based on Church teaching and your own experience, for how we can stay on track and not be confused about what is really important?

"First, we have to have an active prayer life. No matter how good or bad things are, you have to put God first. I like to start and end the day with prayer. These, I think are prerequisites. I even have the Morning Offering framed and hanging in my bathroom. This way I am reminded to offer my day to God before I brush my teeth. The rest of the day, I try to remember that I am offering it to Jesus and try to make it a worthy offering. At the end of the day, I look back in prayer and reflection, giving thanks for what I received and forgiveness for any failings. It is also important each day to ask for God's guidance. Each day we need to turn over control to God. It helps me to have a morning prayer routine. I like to use the morning and evening prayers from the Liturgy of the Hours on my Kindle via the iBreviary app. The morning and evening prayers in the *Magnificat* magazine are also very good (the daily reflections on the Gospel in the *Magnificat* are exceptional). If daily Mass is available to you, take advantage of it. It is not easy to make the time, but there is no place I find more peace than at a reverently said daily Mass. Pray the Rosary or several decades of it. Do this while driving or while exercising if you don't have the time. If you have a family, say a family Rosary at least once a week. Finally, no matter how little time you think you have, you always have time for fifteen to thirty seconds of prayer every time you get into the car before you flip on the radio.

"Second, we know we can't do it alone. That is a very Catholic understanding of faith and salvation. It is not just me and Christ. We are in relationship with God and one another. In reading Scripture, we see that God is not only the God of Abraham, Isaac, and Jacob (people), but the God of Israel. He saves His people. Sure we each can choose to reject God, but if we say yes to His salvation, that means we are now part of something more than just us. So if you are trying to handle your spirituality on your own, you need to stop. That doesn't mean everyone is the same. I have been a part of some groups that drive me up a wall because some things don't work for me. That is fine. We are not all the same. But we need to find a way to connect and be a part of our Christian community. I am part of a Catholic business group, I am a Knight of Columbus, and I am involved with my parish. Some dear friends of mine go to their Cursillo group every week. Others are involved in their prayer groups. Those don't work for me, but work well for them. Find out where you fit.

"Finally, it is important to live deliberately (intentionally). I am trained in psychology, but

> at the end of my training I came to an important realization. Psychology is a field that assumes that behavior is deterministic even in the realm of 'normal' psychology (i.e., we may think we are in control, but our behavior is really determined by a myriad of forces and free will is an illusion). I take the contrary position. I firmly believe that free will is real and one reason that psychology will never be able to completely predict human behavior is that people can choose. However, the reason that psychology can predict human behavior is that people are allowing themselves to be carried along the waves of situations or impulses. We fail to choose to be different. As Catholic men, we must be in touch with God and what He wants, and then we must deliberately choose to be different. Every day we must choose the path."

Of all the great ideas and thoughts you have shared, what would you like any Catholic man reading this book to consider doing immediately to keep their priorities straight?

> "I would want anyone reading this to immediately set down this book and pray. In that prayer, commit yourself to living as a man of virtue who starts with justice that leads to a manly understanding of Christian love. Commit to a daily reflection on what God is asking of you and then surrender to His will every day. Ask Mother Mary to help you become the man you are meant to be. That will mean different things to different men. To some, it may mean letting go of sinful habits. To others it may mean changing how and where they spend their time. For others,

> it may mean seeing their spouse and family in a new light."

Rob's insights and the depth of his answers shed a helpful light on this idea of priorities. As you ponder his words, remember he is the founder of catholicdadsonline.org and interacts with thousands of Catholic men around the world each year. His ideas are not theories, but drawn from Church teaching, his own education and experience, as well as the input from this tremendous web resource.

My next interview is with Rick Swygman. Rick, a convert to the Church in 2001, has been married for twenty-four years and has four wonderful children. He has nearly twenty-five years of experience in financial services sales, sales management, and organizational leadership, serving as a senior leader at Greene Consulting, Bank of America, SunTrust, and Barnett Banks. He is also the executive director of Pinecrest Academy, an independent private Catholic school in the Atlanta area. Rick has a passion for the renewal of authentic Catholic school excellence and the character and moral formation of our youth.

I have enjoyed great conversations with Rick the last few years about our Catholic faith, pursuing what's important and the love we have for our families. Rick is one of the most direct and humble men I know and I am grateful for his contribution to the book.

Rick, as a Catholic father and husband, what are your priorities?

> "Let me first preface this answer acknowledging that although my intent here appears magnanimous, the execution is circumspect due to my own poor efforts. Any 'success,' even just the awareness that the

following *should* be my priorities, is thanks to God. As I understand it, it is more about the fight for holiness and ordering my life toward growing in holiness that matters, more so than the results or 'my success.' As the Gospels and the saints make clear, and from the wonderful understanding of our faith that I have learned since my conversion, if I am willing to be led, I can trust that I can lean on Christ and He will take me by the hand.

"The priorities below were nowhere in sight prior to my conversion in 2001, although I think I was a pretty good guy, good husband, and decent father—at least according to the world's standards. But thanks to all the treasures offered by our faith and the good fortune of being introduced to several of our wonderful papal encyclicals—*Gaudium et spes*, *Laborem exercens*, *Humanae vitae*, *Fides et ratio*, and *The Splendor of Love*—I was able to adjust my priorities fairly early in my marriage while our children were still quite young (*Laborem exercens* completely transformed my view of work, how I worked, and how I led!) These encyclicals, a committed prayer life, the sacraments, frequent spiritual direction, Catholic retreats, and the prayers of my wife helped me to understand better what God and our faith was asking of me.

"So with that, here is finally the answer to your question. I pray that I remain true to these priorities and commitments and carry them out according to God's will.

"*My number one priority* is to lead (by seeking holiness and with the help of God's grace) my family to heaven, and in so doing to bring as many people with us along the way Supporting that overall focus are the following priorities:

1. To love and serve my wife, striving to model a Christ-centered marriage for our children and others.
2. To be a great father for our children, working in partnership with my wife to form them to recognize and fulfill the call that God has for them in their lives.
3. To fully serve in the workplace to advance the 'common good,' bring dignity to all, model and reflect Christ, bring others to Christ and His truth, and in so doing to help the individuals I encounter fulfill their human potential and recognize what God is asking of them.
4. To serve others. While this was previously largely driven through my work at Pinecrest Academy, it is currently mostly carried out through a focus on youth, primarily through coaching youth baseball. I seek to use this as a platform to serve not only the boys, but also the families around them (as most of the teams I coach have at least 50 percent of their families divorced or in some way broken).

"Although these are my priorities, being able to live them out is another story! To best do so, my daily commitment is to strive with God's grace to grow in holiness, knowing that I cannot do any of this without Him. So to best accomplish this, I fully engage in the following commitments:

- Morning Offering or greeting (first thing as I roll out of bed onto my knees)
- Rosary on the way to Adoration
- Thirty minutes of Adoration on the north end of town before heading to work
- Thirty-minute Gospel meditation before Mass (once I get to the south end of town)
- Daily Mass
- Prayer to St. Joseph at the beginning of the day
- Little prayers throughout the day—even trying to make my day a form of prayer itself
- Evening examination prior to bedtime
- Twice per week holy hour
- Confession every two or three weeks
- Annual two or three day silent retreat
- All throughout seeking to have a personal 'relationship' with Christ (my greatest challenge being to just sit and talk to Him and listen to Him!)"

Does this list and the way you choose to live your life require difficult choices? Please explain.

"Prior to my conversion and a growing understanding of Christ and our faith, I would have said yes, this definitely calls for difficult choices and takes way too much time out of the day. But when I started committing to these things early after my conversion, I found that my days were actually more productive and definitely more fulfilling. So today I would not call it difficult, but rather a fulfilling exercise of sacrifice and *detachment*. I have faith that Christ *will* reward our fidelity, which changes it from something 'difficult' to something so worth it. God has helped me to see the value and meaning in such sacrifice, and how self-sacrifice for Him, my wife, my children, and others is at the core of true love.

"I know the list of commitments above may seem over the top to some people, but without them I would be lost. This 'way of life' gives me a great sense of peace knowing that if I remain true to these priorities, I can leave the results to God.

"With my greatest weakness being selfishness, learning and aligning to the Catholic faith via prayer, sacraments, confession, spiritual direction, has helped me better recognize this weakness and seek to root it out. God has clearly shown me the gifts that come from selflessness, detachment, and sacrifice, and how it helps so with my priorities. While I lose sight of this frequently, thanks to the practice of our faith I am able to recognize it and respond.

"I have also found that these sacrifices, commitments, and priorities, coupled with God's grace, have in many ways become inspirational to others whom I encounter through work and daily life. Just living these out and following God's will as much as possible seems to often lead others to stop, reflect, and sometimes even change."

What would be the impact on your family and your own Catholic faith if you chose to place your work, acquiring things you don't need, and the expectations of the world before Christ and your family?

"The impact clearly would not be good, leaving me at the mercy of my own abilities, rather than God's grace! I believe this is at the core of so many of the problems we encounter in our culture today. My family would easily recognize and be forced to adjust to the fact that work is the priority, and that they come second to that. I have so often seen (particularly when I worked at Pinecrest Academy) the impact on spouses and children from a father who holds work and material success as his top priority. They yearn for so much more from their husband or father, and clearly suffer when it falls short. Materialism and relativism take over, as does a yearning for attention, seeking to fill the gaps that exist from a father who does not have the family and their faith as the priority. While I still am prone to acquire things I don't need (and am working on this, particularly after reading a great book by Father Thomas Dubay, *Happy Are You Poor*), my family is so much happier due to a stronger focus on what is truly meaningful and lasting, versus material items and worldly success. I have a wonderful wife to thank for this! She is completely detached from materialism, worldly success, and how others may judge us. So while she wanted this for our family, she had to wait for me to come along to bring it to life and to our children.

"A brief personal story to share here that relates to this question. About nine years ago, just after my conversion to the Catholic faith, thanks to a powerful moment in prayer that I will never forget, I concluded that I needed to resign from my role as an executive leader at Bank of America. After months of daily Adoration and prayer asking God what He wanted of me, I finally announced my 'retirement' from Bank of America, informing my team that because of my faith and my family I was moving on to something that better aligned with my priorities as a husband and a father. (We had two children in elementary school at the time, and just adopted our two younger children.) Although I had not yet concluded what I was going to do, this process ultimately led me to Atlanta to become executive director at Pinecrest Academy, which perfectly aligned to my mission and that of our family.

"I was soon shocked to see the response from my announcement. Word spread throughout the entire company and even through the industry. I can't tell you how many calls I received from men (fathers and husbands) who wanted to understand what I was doing and why I was doing it. On a few occasions, the men who called me broke down in tears expressing their great regret at having missed the opportunity to do the same for their families before their kids were grown and left home. And at least one senior executive who learned of this decided to make a similar change in life, taking this as a sign or inspiration that he needed to adjust his own priorities for the good of his family.

"I never expected this reaction, and subsequently realized what God could do with detachment from 'worldly' success, a focus on Him, and living out the priorities to which He calls us."

Do the men you encounter every day have their priorities in order? If not, why?

"Sadly, the majority don't. As mentioned above, I think this is the greatest contributor to the social and societal ills we face today. So many men I encounter through work life (traveling throughout the country in my job and daily life outside of work) do not have the right priorities. I say this, not judgmentally but sincerely, recognizing that due to our fallen nature even those of us 'committed to our faith' are always just one step away from losing sight of the right priorities and falling prey to the consequences of a lukewarm faith, worldly attachments, and sin.

"Most of the men I encounter are so swallowed up by the world's view of success, that is, great job, trophy wife (or wives), lavish lifestyle, super successful and popular kids they can brag about—all driven by pride, selfishness, vanity, and laziness, as I am! But most are either without Christ in their lives to counter it all, or lukewarm in their faith, leaving them prone to shallow lives rife with materialism, relativism, and great pain within the family ultimately leading to divorce, broken children, immodesty, promiscuity, and so on.

"So the short answer is, the men I encounter do not have the right priorities in order, and the reason why is due to the powerful influence of the world, riches, fame, and a lack of faith and Christ as the priority in their lives. Seeing this so consistently has helped me recognize that without a life of prayer and the sacraments, I am also one step away from losing sight of the right priorities and falling prey to the same."

If you could speak candidly to a group of young Catholic men, including your own sons, what would you like to say to them about the choices they will have to make in life?

"I fortunately have been given several opportunities to speak to other men, particularly young men. The messages I try to convey fall right in line with the questions you are asking and the book you are writing. I encourage them to reflect on what truly matters in life and to seek to understand *their purpose in life*, that is, God's plan for them, and to follow His will, not their own or anyone else's.

"The key point I try to convey through stories and examples is the power of understanding and following God's will, and the value of serving others and giving of themselves. True happiness and fulfillment comes from self-giving. Nothing compares to the sense of joy and fulfillment that comes from that. And to do that, we need to know and understand Christ, the model of selfless giving for others. The Catholic faith provides the perfect guide to do this, recognizing the dignity of every individual, the power of self-giving, and the power of the Cross.

"More practically, I encourage them (if married) to love their wives, and love and lead their families based on their understanding of and love for Christ, and keeping Him at the center. Nothing will provide them more lasting fulfillment and meaning when they come to the end of their lives.

"I often use the story of my kidney donation here, as it is a story of profound joy, happiness, and conversion, and what it has done for others as a result. I hesitated doing so at one time due to a fear of appearing prideful, but my spiritual guide, Father Todd Belardi, directed me to set my vanity aside and tell the story without hesitation, suggesting that God would do great things with it, which has proven to be true. This typically launches into a discussion about the opportunities to give selflessly in so many small ways throughout the day, and how that leads to happiness and fulfillment.

"Randy, there are five events in my life that I can look at as the most powerful acts of God's grace in my life. If for some reason you want more insight as to those and the impact they have had on me and others, let me know. These five events are:

- My conversion
- My decision to change careers (story in the second question above)

- Our adoption
- The kidney donation
- Our two oldest children serving as missionaries (and how they and their experience led our family to an even stronger faith)

"In the end, I pray that my fidelity and integrity in my commitments to faith, family, work, and others, in big and small matters, will, through God's grace and Mary's and Joseph's intercession, aid me in fulfilling God's will for me and draw others to know, love, and serve Christ."

Rob Kaiser and Rick Swygman have provided us with a plethora of ways to address what is important with specific actions rooted in Church teaching. As we consider how we will live our lives each day, starting now, what are we prepared to do differently? It is important to hear from other Catholic men who may lead lives similar to your own or maybe at one time were where you are in life. Take this to prayer. Study our faith. Seek out other faithful Catholic men as mentors, guides, and accountability partners. Let's go.

QUESTIONS FOR REFLECTION

1. Do I struggle in the area of knowing what's important? Do I have a sense of regret or guilt because of areas of my life not receiving enough time or attention? What am I prepared to do differently?

2. Rob Kaiser offered a more psychological and big picture view of priorities laced with real life and Catholic teaching while Rick Swygman was straightforward and very practical through the prism of what the Church and Scripture teach us. Can I see the value both men offered? Can I find nuggets of wisdom in their advice to help me gain focus and clarity?
3. The author wrote, "We spend so much time trying to manage or stay ahead of the burdens of the life we have created that we don't make time for Jesus." Is this true for me? Have I built a life that is requiring too much of me to support and maintain?
4. Can I list all of my activities for tomorrow, based on aligning my priorities the way I have learned in this chapter and with knowing Christ is first, family second, and work third? What would this list look like? Can it become a personal road map to keep me focused?

CHAPTER SIXTEEN

True Catholic Rebels

If we are going to be rebels, let's rebel against the world
and embrace the path to heaven
that leads through the Catholic Church.
— Author —

Come on guys, we know better than the Church, don't we? After all, this is the twenty-first century and times have changed. Modern man is fully capable of deciding what is moral on his own, right? All the really smart people in the media, government, and academia who encourage us to embrace abortion, contraception, euthanasia, and gay marriage can't be wrong, can they? After all, everyone knows that new and fresh ideas must clearly trump over two millennia of Church teaching. Right?

Wrong.

Unfortunately, my facetious opening paragraph represents how many Catholics view the Church's teaching these days.

Many have bought into the lies the world is feeding us, that we should rebel against the authority of the Church and the pope, deciding on our own which teachings we will and will not follow. Our increasing apathy and moral relativism, heavily influenced by a culture drunk on materialism with no moral compass, is putting the Church and the world in grave danger. The Catholic Church is one of the last lines of defense against evil and we must not allow a misguided rebellion to destroy it from the inside. The Church must never conform to, or be assimilated into, the world. We are in the world but not of the world, and we must keep our eyes firmly on our heavenly home.

TRUE CATHOLIC REBELS

Men, if we feel the need to be rebellious, why not send this energy in a more positive direction, a direction that leads to heaven? It is easy to criticize the Church and conform to the world's various influences, but perhaps today's true Catholic rebel can stand out by embracing Church teaching, not rejecting it, and following the pope's leadership, not undermining it. If we want to truly follow Christ's teachings, shouldn't we do so through the very Church He founded? If we are going to be rebels, let's rebel against the world and embrace the path to heaven that leads through the Catholic Church.

SIX POSITIVE WAYS FOR CATHOLIC MEN TO REBEL AGAINST THE WORLD

1. **Avoid cafeteria Catholicism.** We can't pick and choose what we believe and still be authentically Catholic. Follow the magisterium and authentically practice our faith, trusting that two millennia of

Church history and teaching are far superior to what we may come up with on our own.

2. **Put our pride aside and surrender.** Think about our exploration of this topic in chapter two. It must take a pretty big ego to say no to Christ and His Church! What we need is more humility, total surrender, and a sincere commitment to put Christ's will before our own. I know from personal experience that doing it my way has never really worked out well.

3. **Restore manhood.** Fight society's war against manhood by being a true man of God. We are being belittled, marginalized, and emasculated from every angle and we must fight back. Stand up for what the people attacking manhood despise. Be a real husband to your wife. Be a great father to your children. Be the spiritual leader at home. Lift up and support the Sacrament of Marriage through the testimony of your own solid marriage. Be a man unafraid to share Christ with others and answer the call to evangelize.

4. **Practice personal holiness.** In *Christifideles laici*, no. 16, St. Pope John Paul II states: "The call to holiness is *rooted in Baptism* and proposed anew in the other Sacraments, principally in the *Eucharist*. Since Christians are reclothed in Christ Jesus and refreshed by his Spirit, they are 'holy.' They therefore have the ability to manifest this holiness and the responsibility to bear witness to it in all that they do. The apostle Paul never tires

of admonishing all Christians to live 'as is fitting among saints' (Eph 5:3)."

5. **Be joyful!** It is so easy to get lost in our problems and forget to be joyful—it happens to me and just about everyone else I know. But remember that we are surrounded by people who are watching us. They may be seeking Him and looking for someone, anyone, to show them the way to Christ. They could learn from our good example, be inspired by our joy, and be encouraged by our faith journey if we will only remember that we are called to share the Good News. If we are gloomy, frustrated, inward-focused, and critical of the Church we will never be able to help anyone and may put our own salvation at risk.
6. **Pursue heaven, reject the world.** This is core to the book and a message we must remember! Heaven is our ultimate destination and not this place called Earth. Will our critics help us get to heaven? Will they stand up for us during tough times? No, they will pull us into a secular way of life that has little room for God and where materialism and popularity are the fashionable idols of the day. Doing what is right is not always easy, but in the long run it is clearly the most beneficial. Why would we not choose heaven?

There is still another way to be a true Catholic rebel in today's world that is the thread which runs through all the other acts I mentioned: *pray faithfully every day.*

As we have learned throughout this book, start the day with a prayer of thanks to God for the blessings in our lives. Pray for help and courage to face the trials the world throws at us. Make the Sign of the Cross and pray over every meal, public or private. Pray a daily Rosary or five decades of it and ask for the help and intercession of our Blessed Mother, and pray with our families every night. I can't envision anyone seriously rebelling against the Church if they are faithfully committed to daily prayer.

It would be easy to read this chapter and decide that it doesn't apply to us, but I would suggest we are all guilty of some degree of negative rebellion each day. Think of all the missed opportunities we have had to be the light of Christ to others. We may take the easy way out in the practice of our faith when a little extra effort is required or we ignore what is required by our God-given vocations. We may push back against doing what we know to be right because we fear the negative opinions of others or lack the courage to confront difficult situations.

One of the things I found most attractive about the Catholic Church when I converted was that it is not easy to be Catholic. I grew up with "easy faith" in the Baptist Church as a young man, left as a teenager, and had no faith at all for twenty-three years until coming home to the truth of Catholicism in 2005. I am incredibly grateful for my Catholic faith and don't see why I should waste my time arguing against the teachings of the Church. I already spent over two decades saying no to God, and my pride-filled rebellion was exhausting. When I surrendered to His will in 2005 I started saying yes, and that has made all the difference in my life.

I have long admired the ministry work of Crossing the Goal and their work with Catholic men. As I thought and prayed about possible men to interview for this chapter, I knew I wanted someone from this ministry and a chance referral from a mutual friend led me to Peter Herbeck.

Peter Herbeck is the vice president and director of Missions for Renewal Ministries. He has been actively involved in evangelization and Catholic renewal throughout the United States, Canada, Africa, Asia, Latin America, and Eastern Europe for the past twenty-five years. Peter co-hosts "The Choices We Face," and is a member of Crossing the Goal. He also daily hosts a dynamic radio program, Fire on the Earth, focusing on Catholic mission and evangelization. He is the author of two recent books, *When the Spirit Comes in Power* and *When the Spirit Speaks*, as well as an inspirational CD series entitled "The True Discipleship Series." Peter also serves on the Board of the National Fellowship of Catholic Men and is a frequent conference speaker. He holds a BA in philosophy from the University of St. Thomas and an MA in theology from Sacred Heart Major Seminary in Detroit.

Peter and his wife of twenty-two years, Debbie, have four children, Sarah (twenty-one), Michael (twenty), Joshua (sixteen) and Rachel (fourteen). Peter and his family are members of Christ the King parish in Ann Arbor.

Peter, through your work with Crossing the Goal and Renewal Ministries, what kind of examples do you observe most Catholic men setting for their families, friends, and coworkers? What are the biggest contributors to what you are seeing?

> "Most men I speak to and observe would acknowledge that they are missing the mark when it comes to spiritual leadership in life and family. Most Catholic men are in need of basic conversion. The kind of

conversion St. Pope John Paul II spoke about in *Redemptoris missio* is that conversion begins with a 'faith which is total and radical' and leads men to 'accepting, by a personal decision, the saving sovereignty of Christ and becoming his disciple' (no. 46).

"Most men do not see themselves, nor understand what it means to live as Jesus' disciple. Many have yet to come to know Jesus in a personal way. As a result they often feel lost when it comes to spiritual things. The call, by the Church, to men to live out their baptism each day, as priest, prophet, and king escapes them. Few men know how to pray, to communicate the faith, or to use the gifts the Lord has given them to make present His kingdom in the world.

"Because they haven't come into a mature, adult relationship with Christ in His Church, they don't engage the mission they have been given to lead their families, to make their home a domestic church. As a result, few men seem to be able to do something as simple as leading family prayer. Prayer, when it happens, falls to Mom by default. Dad's uncomfortable, so he follows rather than leads.

"He can't lead with confidence because he hasn't built the basic foundations into his own life. He's not motivated to rise to the challenge; he doesn't know what to do. Simple, essential building blocks are missing: daily prayer, reading of Scripture, frequent reception of the sacraments, generous giving, and a commitment to mission, evangelization, and so on.

"As a result he experiences his spiritual life as a form of religion. It's boring, mostly about rules that are hard to follow, and he's often plagued by a nagging sense of guilt. The whole Church thing is unpleasant, uncomfortable, and awkward.

"Lots of guys live on an island when it comes to spiritual things and their interior life. They carry their burdens, fears, sins, temptations, and failings on their own. Many men are trapped in habitual patterns of sin, living double lives. They often keep spiritual things and the mission of the Church at arms-length because they feel unworthy, inadequate, or hypocritical. Who am I to say anything to anyone else? Better not to say anything at all. Because they don't open their lives, the Church doesn't reach them at their point of need. They then, too often, conclude that they 'don't get anything out of being Catholic.'

"Younger men don't have too many models to inspire them to a radical and integrated life of discipleship. How many successful Catholic businessmen do they know who can speak freely about their relationship with Jesus and what being in the Church means to them? Pope Francis described Catholic life as a 'community in mission,' and the baptized as 'disciples in mission' who live their lives in a 'perpetual state of mission.' Where do young men see such men?

"Most of the young adult men we encounter are having a difficult timing growing up, coming into manhood. The culture attempts to addict them to prolonged adolescence, which includes avoiding commitment, keeping ones options open at all times, playing games, putting off marriage in order to remain 'free' as long as possible, and making sure to maximize their fun while they still can. Children, family responsibilities, living for the good of others, making real sacrifices, living under the lordship of Jesus seem too confining, suffocating, and limiting. To take up ones cross is to miss all the fun.

"There are heroic exceptions to all of this, but the statistics tell the story. Nearly every poll shows how large percentages of baptized Catholic men live no differently than their peers who don't believe in God."

Much has been written about the "emasculation of men" in today's society. Do you think that is contributing to some of the challenging examples you are seeing among our Catholic men?

"Yes. The secular culture around us is at war with the authentically masculine. The obliteration of gender is one example of it. Hollywood works overtime undermining the role of men and fathers. Fathers are normally depicted in sitcoms and the like as buffoons—weak, out of touch, unable to lead, self-centered, perpetually adolescent.

"Cultural norms and customs for men and women have changed dramatically. Society today rewards and even idolizes the self-centered, narcissistic male set on reaching personal fulfillment. The point of life is self-fulfillment, which necessitates defining reality, the good life, the meaning and purpose of life on my own terms.

"Jesus calls every man to die to self. He calls every man to become a warrior, to lay down his life for others. Healthy men know that life is not about them, that authentic manhood is found in providing for others, in protecting, leading, forming, and guiding the next generation.

"The emasculated male is at war with his own heart. Every young man, every healthy young man, wants to become a man in the true sense. He wants to be brave, to do something heroic and meaningful with his life. In his true heart he wants to lose himself and to take up the responsibilities God has placed before him. He wants to bear great responsibilities with dignity and live a life worthy of respect. Though most men cannot articulate it, they want to follow Jesus to Calvary. Emasculation kills, or at least severely weakens, this innate desire by training men to be preoccupied with saving their own lives. To be Catholic means just the opposite."

How does a Catholic man go about setting the right example for others? What does this mean in very practical terms?

"St. Paul captures what I think is the first step in the following verse of Scripture: *I have been crucified with Christ; it is no longer I who live, but Christ who lives in me; and the life I now live in the flesh I live by faith in the Son of God, who loved me and gave himself for me* (Galatians 2:20–21).

"Step one has to be a decision of the heart to imitate Jesus and to live for Him. We won't do it perfectly, but unless we consciously choose it and make it our overriding passion and purpose, we won't know how to set the right example.

"Next, put into place those simple habits that will allow the Lord to form His character in you. Decide to set aside time each day to pray. Prayer is conversation with God. This will be the foundation of your life as His disciple. He wants to speak to you, to reveal Himself to you, to reveal His plan and purpose for your life. He will teach you how to set an example for others.

"An important piece of your conversation with God is the daily reading of the Bible. Pope Emeritus Benedict XVI said he believed that the secret to a 'new spiritual springtime' for the Church could be found in the 'daily reading of the word of God.' Why? He said because Jesus is present on every page of Scripture, He's waiting to speak to us, to form us in His image. We can't imitate Him or set an example for others if we don't know who He is. St. Jerome said it best: 'Ignorance of Scripture is ignorance of Christ.' Many men have no idea how to set a Christ-like example for others because they don't know Him.

"Frequent reception of the sacraments is also important. Mass attendance every Sunday is the minimum. Daily prayer and weekly Mass attendance are fundamental ways to start setting the right example. Let your children, family, and friends see how much your relationship with Jesus really matters to you. Put first things first, honor the Lord's Day without compromise. Make it a non-negotiable, not just because it's a sin not to, but because you want to!

"As you begin to walk with the Lord, He will change you. Your priorities will change; you'll find yourself wanting to please Him first in all that you do. It won't all happen at once nor will you do it perfectly, but you will change, one step at a time.

"One of the most practical things you can do to set an example for others is to actually live by the golden rule: treat others the way you would like to be treated. Ask yourself, in your marriage, in relating to your children, when confronting a problem at work, or just relating to colleagues, how would I want to be treated in this situation? If you do you'll find yourself doing what the Scriptures call you to do. For example, to be quick to hear and slow to speak, to say only the things men need to hear, to count others better than yourself, to humble yourself, to not let the sun go down on your anger, to be angry but not to sin, to speak the truth in love, to forgive as you've been forgiven, to be sober, to not get drunk, to love your enemies, to put away anger, wrath, malice, slander, and foul talk from your mouth, to control your own body in holiness and honor, and so on."

Earlier in this chapter I referred to the critical importance of letting those around us see our joy and the "light of Christ" at work in our lives in an effort to rebel against the world. Do you agree?

"Yes. And it's important to remember that to express the joy of the Lord is not simply a feeling, but a decision that is based upon the unchanging truth of what Jesus Christ has done for you. God loves you. He has sent His Son to die for you so that you might become a child of God, an heir to the kingdom and glory of God! Let the world know that you possess, by God's mercy, the pearl of great price. Your life, no matter what you experience today, no matter what trials you encounter, what disappointments come your way, nothing can separate you from the love of God. In Christ you have been given a kingdom, eternal life, the fulfillment of all your desire. We have reason to rejoice!

"This is the central point of Pope Francis' new Apostolic Exhortation, *Evangelii gaudium,* 'The Joy of the Gospel.'

"What difference does knowing Jesus make? Joy has a force of attraction. The joy that attracts is a fruit that comes from living with Jesus in the Holy Spirit. It's a reality the world does not know and cannot produce. This is why it's so important to let the joy of the Lord radiate from our lives or become the 'light of Christ' as you appropriately named it. People need to see it.

"What does the Christian possess that an unbeliever would want? As one author put it, 'If I become a Christian am I trading up or trading down?' Joy is a treasure everyone longs to possess. Let your light shine. Show others what is possible for their own lives.

"Far too many Catholic men rarely demonstrate the joy of the Lord. Even at Mass men often look bored and distracted, or as Pope Francis put it, like they 'just came from a funeral.' Joy is one of the defining characteristics of new life in Christ. If we don't have it, it's a sure sign that we have yet to encounter Jesus and to know Him as He desires to be known."

If the readers of this book are inspired to seek out good examples to follow or desire to be better role models themselves, what would you say to them? What would be the next steps?

"First, read the lives of the saints. They are our models. These are men and women, ordinary men and women, whose lives were transformed by Jesus. They show us what is possible, what God wants to produce in us.

"Second, I would find a Godly man in my parish, someone who is walking the walk, a man of holiness and integrity. Proverbs tell us when we find such a man we should wear out his door step. Find out what makes him tick, what the Lord has shown him about being an example for others. How has he navigated the challenges in the work place, among his peers and colleagues? Where does he find his strength?

> "Third, I would find a small band of brothers, other men who want to 'go all in' as disciples of Jesus. Find men who are willing to put their cards on the table, men who want what you want. Share your lives with one another, the good and the bad. Learn to pray together, to study God's Word together, help one another through difficult times. If you find such a band willing to open your lives to one another and to follow the Lord wherever He leads, He will guide you, and will give you wisdom and discernment as you seek to be His man in the world. Every man needs the strength that comes from such a brotherhood. It's an integral part of discipleship. We are not meant to fight alone."

As Peter shared, we can't do this alone and we must pray for the guidance of the Holy Spirit. In my own experience, this is a daily work in progress and it is never easy. But we should all recognize that there are people looking at us to see our example. They want to learn from and be inspired by our courage, if we are only willing to take a stand for Christ. Think about how fortunate we are to live in a Christian country (although our religious liberties are under attack) where all we risk is possible disapproval or alienation from others. When we take our faith to work and out into the public square, we are standing up to that fear and solidifying the core values that we as Christians believe in. It will be difficult at times and will require sacrifice, but to live with the love of God every minute of every day is far more rewarding than a little disapproval.

I know this is difficult, but the sacrifice on our part is required. The sacrifice is simply to love Christ more than we love the opinions of those around us, and set an example worth emulating. Let's pray for one another and continue to ask Jesus for strength and the discernment to know and follow His will. Tomorrow is a new day. Will we have the courage to be a light for Christ to those around us?

Have you ever seen a picture of St. Michael the Archangel standing over a defeated Lucifer? In Milton's *Paradise Lost*, Lucifer declared his rebellion in heaven against God with the cry, "*Non serviam*!" (from the Latin, "I will not serve!"). The Archangel Michael loyally defended God with his cry of "*Serviam*," and vanquished Lucifer to hell with all his demons.

Brothers, what will it be for us, *Serviam* or *Non serviam*?

QUESTIONS FOR REFLECTION

1. Have I ever been guilty of the "bad" rebellion described by the author in the opening paragraph?
2. The author has shared in this chapter and several times in the book that we are made for heaven and not this world. What does that mean to me? Am I on the path that leads to heaven?
3. The author and Peter Herbeck carefully explained the importance of joy and the attraction joy holds for others. Does my relationship with Christ and living out my faith make me experience joy? Am I a joyful "light of Christ" to those around me? Why or why not?
4. Am I actively doing any of the six ways to be a positive Catholic rebel from the author's list? Where do I fall short? Am I ready to commit to living this way and rebelling against the world?

Conclusion

I have fought the good fight, I have finished the race,
I have kept the faith. From now on there is laid up for me
the crown of righteousness, which the Lord, the righteous
judge, will award to me on that Day, and not only to me but
also to all who have loved his appearing.
— 2 Timothy 4:7–8 —

Have you ever wondered if you will have the opportunity to tell the people you love all that you want them to know about what is important in life and convey important life lessons? How many of us have benefited from the influence of our fathers, grandfathers, and other important people in our lives? Out of my strong desire to raise my sons to be strong and faithful Catholic men, I have composed a letter to them which I hope inspires you to do something similar with your children and grandchildren. Our children and future generations will not know Christ or our Catholic faith unless we share our experiences, wisdom and perhaps some of what we may have gleaned from this book. Please reflect and pray on this serious responsibility . . . for their sake as well as our own.

My Dear Sons,

It must seem strange that I am writing specifically to you at the end of this book. When you finish reading this you will hopefully understand the reason. I want you to know your mom and I love you both very much and we could not be prouder of you. We are not perfect parents, but we have done our best to help you make your way through these difficult growing-up years and prepare for the future.

As I've grown older I have gained a sense of perspective and am grateful for the ability to reflect on the many lessons I have experienced. I appreciate the challenges I have encountered because they have helped to shape me as a man, husband, and father. I wish I could remember all of the wisdom my parents shared with me when I was your age, but I can only catch fleeting memories every now and then as the years pass.

There is so much I wish to share with you! I want to tell you what it feels like to fall in love with the woman you will marry. I want you to know the indescribable joy I felt when both of you came into this world. I want you to understand the rough years I spent in the spiritual wilderness with no faith and the profound conversion experience I had when I surrendered to Christ and found the truth I was seeking for most of my life in the Catholic Church. The list of rich experiences and lessons is almost endless . . . but perhaps I will share some of them now and save the rest for future books.

To keep it simple, here are eight things I want you to think about, pray over, and hopefully remember for the rest of your lives:

1. FAITH. God loves you, no matter what. Stay true to yourself and always love and serve Him. Stay devoted to our Catholic faith despite all the temptations you will have from the world to leave. Be men of prayer and observe the sacraments, especially the Eucharist and Reconciliation. *Never forget* you were made for heaven and not the world.
2. VALUES. Your mom and I have taught you the difference between right and wrong. Our Catholic faith has helped you learn to love your neighbor and serve others. Never lose touch with your values—they define who you are. Don't be tempted to sacrifice your values for a little temporary comfort or pleasure. It is never, ever worth it.
3. EDUCATION. School isn't always going to be fun. It wasn't for us either. But, it is very important to have a quality education if you want to have good career options. Never be satisfied that you know enough. Become lifelong learners, not only in school, but also about our beautiful Catholic faith. Be insatiably curious about other people and life in general.
4. WORK ETHIC. Nothing in life is truly free. Work hard and you will be rewarded. Pay your dues and out hustle everyone around you. No matter what you hear later in life, I promise you there is no easy path to riches and there is no substitute for hard work. I know, I know, this part sounds just like Papa!

5. **Love.** You will meet lots and lots of girls in your lives. Treat them all with dignity and respect. Care more about their inner beauty than their outward appearance. Treat your bodies like holy temples and don't give in to sinful behavior. You will know you are in love when your knees go soft, your stomach has butterflies, and you can't stop thinking about her as the most beautiful girl you have ever seen. Then what? Get to know her, build a relationship, and take the time to see if she is the *one*. You will eventually know if she is and she will be looking at you the same way. Be countercultural, do the right thing, and save yourselves for marriage. The world might make fun of you, but Jesus will love you for it.

6. **Responsibility.** You have heard your mom and I say this a million times: "You need to be more responsible!" Well, you do. Someone has to be responsible, why not you? If you are involved in an activity or project, act responsible and be a leader. If you make a mess, clean it up. If you say you will do something, do it. One of my old bosses told me years ago that if "I touched it, I owned it!" This has always served me well and helped me in countless ways. Don't wait for somebody else to take responsibility. It may be up to you. By the way, do you know who is *always* responsible for your actions? You.

7. **Friendships.** Be true to yourself and your friends. Hang out with people who share your values. Be a good enough friend to others that you always tell

them the truth. This is the sign of a true friend. If your friends go down a path you know is wrong, stand your ground and do not follow. The tricky thing about friendships is you sometimes find yourself alone because you are committed to following the teachings of the Church or the values you learned as young people. Trust me on this one—*never abandon your faith or your values to follow the crowd.* On the other hand, you will hopefully have a few close friends who stay with you a lifetime and they are to be treasured as gifts from God.

8. **Be Real.** Don't ever pretend to be someone else. You are who God created you to be. Don't be tempted to hide your true self, your faith, or what you really think from others.

I hope you read this and come to me with lots of questions. I promise that I (and your mom) are always here to help you. Did you know your mom and I have a vocation (job) given to us by God? Our vocation is to help our family (and everyone else) get to heaven. That is our number one responsibility as parents. You are going to stumble and struggle at times in life, but always remember we are here for you and we love you. Most importantly, God loves you and He will never abandon you. He wants you to learn, grow, and think for yourselves, but never stray from His love.

Boys, I want you to be happy. Really, truly happy! You know what? You can't be truly happy unless you have joy. Do you know where joy comes from? Joy comes from putting Christ first in your lives and loving Him so much that everyone sees

Him at work inside you. Then, you will have true joy, which will make you really and truly happy.

Did you notice the Scripture passage at the top of this letter? Reflect on the beginning of the passage: *I have competed well; I have finished the race; I have kept the faith.* One day, when you are husbands and fathers with children of your own, I pray you will say these words to me . . . and pass these lessons on to your own children.

One more thing . . . I wrote this book for you.

— With all my love, Dad —

APPENDIX ONE

How Pornography Destroys Lives

AN INTERVIEW WITH PATRICK TRUEMAN, PRESIDENT OF MORALITY IN MEDIA

Knowing pornography was a rapidly growing problem for men, I reached out to a Catholic expert named Patrick Trueman, President of Morality in Media, to get his insights on the problem and what men can do to shake this evil addiction. Patrick is the president and CEO of Morality in Media. A member of St. Francis Xavier Council 6608 in Buffalo, Minnesota, he served as chief of the U.S. Department of Justice Child Exploitation and Obscenity Section, Criminal Division, under Presidents Ronald Reagan and George H.W. Bush.

Patrick, through your work as President of Morality in Media and a lifetime spent fighting against obscenity, indecency, pornography, and sexually oriented businesses, how would you describe the impact pornography is having on men today, specifically Catholic men? Do you have any statistics you can share?

"Every Catholic priest I talk to tells me that pornography is the number one problem mentioned in Confession, and remember, only the most devout men are going to Confession.

"There is a wealth of information on our peer-reviewed research site that contains statistics on porn use. See PornHarmsResearch.com or http://pornharmsresearch.com/2012/07/teens-and-college-students-the-epidemic-of-pornography-use-in-america-statistics/. Some of these numbers indicating the use of porn are quite low in my opinion but they all indicate that porn use is widespread. The consumption of pornography begins at a much earlier age for most users today than ever before, due to the Internet accessibility of pornography. The images are 'harder' and much more deviant than was available a generation ago when only *Playboy* magazine was available to relatively few youths.

"The volume of material consumed by children is vastly greater than a generation or so ago also. Then a child might get hold of a single magazine that might have a dozen photos of topless women. Today, a child is accessing hundreds and thousands of photos and videos of hardcore, often violent, and certainly deviant pornography. Child pornography is also accessed. Thus, before reaching adulthood, the Catholic or other person is steeped in pornographic deviance that often becomes the dominant influence in their life, replacing family, school, friendships, and church / religion. There is research indicating that a growing number of twenty-something men suffer from 'porn-induced sexual dysfunction,' according to *Psychology Today*. These men cannot think about or do not want to think about marriage or family life—it is just not of interest to them.

"The Catholic Church (or any church) has little chance of evangelizing these people—it's extremely difficult to compete with the messages received from pornography."

How do Catholic men fall into the "pornography trap"? What draws them in?

"Almost all are drawn in as children today. This should provide a clue on how to prevent or at least curb this problem. While some think it is inappropriate to have church or school programs on the topic of pornography directed at children, exposure to porn begins in grade school for almost all children and they are not the least prepared to deal with it. Curiosity and peer pressure, the easy availability of Internet pornography, and the addictive nature of pornography trap these people. Also, many children fall into the trap because parents are so uneducated on the ways to protect against pornography. A small percentage of families have blocking software and

> those that do have it only on one device in the home. It needs to be on all Internet-enabled devices. Also, parents are not aware of monitoring software that allows them to see which sites their children visit. Blocking and monitoring software should be used for adults as well to prevent temptation. We live in a sexualized culture with a porn shop within reach at all times. It might be a desktop computer, a laptop, a cell phone, or an iPad."

Do you have any examples in mind of Catholic marriages and families torn apart by porn addiction?

> "I don't have any specifics to mention but wives who have lost their husbands to porn contact us at MIM every day."

What are concrete steps Catholic men of all ages can take to avoid pornography? Would you recommend St. Pope John Paul II's Theology of the Body as the key Catholic teaching to help men understand the beautiful gifts God has given us in our bodies, the loving relationship with our wives, and the Sacrament of Marriage?

> "I would of course recommend JP II's critical work but in reality most men will not read it. Men need to understand *what pornography does to them* because it is unfortunately true that most will not be motivated by what porn does to others, such as wives or girlfriends, but rather by what it does to them. They need to understand that pornography profoundly alters brain function in much the same way that cocaine does. Many avoid illicit drugs because they do

not want to suffer addiction, but few know that porn causes an addiction that is little different than that and just as debilitating as that caused by cocaine. In fact, many clinicians will tell you that a porn addiction is harder to overcome because you can't detox like you can with cocaine or alcohol—the material is stored *right in the brain* and thus can be recalled easily. Also, our sexualized society presents many 'triggers' for recalling pornography that has been viewed. Since that material is stored in the brain, one need not go buy pornography to relapse and in that way it is different than for example a cocaine addiction.

"I also recommend frequent confession (weekly) and Communion, daily, if at all possible. We cannot overlook the great spiritual help, the rivers of graces, that is offered to us by the Catholic faith to overcome sin."

If a Catholic man is reading this interview and realizes they have succumbed to porn addiction or they are heading down that road, what would be your counsel on how to break free? Where can they seek immediate help?

"Frequent confession and Communion, an experienced counselor who works with pornography addicted individuals, blocking software, monitoring software, and a good friend to work with to rid the person of their porn collection."

AUTHOR'S NOTE: ADDITIONAL INFORMATION AND RESOURCES

- The *Catechism of the Catholic Church* states, "Pornography . . . offends against chastity because it perverts the conjugal act, the intimate giving of spouses to each other. It does grave injury to the dignity of its participants (actors, vendors, the public), since each one becomes an object of base pleasure and illicit profit for others" (2354).
- The website for Morality in Media (MIM) is www.moralityinmedia.org. Morality in Media also hosts another website—pornharms.com—that offers peer-reviewed research on the harm of pornography and resources to protect men and their families from these harms.
- The Knights of Columbus Catholic Information Service makes available in booklet form *Blessed Are The Pure In Heart: A Pastoral Letter on the Dignity of the Human Person and the Dangers of Pornography* [http://www.kofc.org/un/en/resources/cis/cis323.pdf] (2007) by Bishop Robert W. Finn of Kansas City-St. Joseph, Missouri. To request the booklet, visit kofc.org/cis.
- Emmaus Road Publishing's upcoming book to be released in 2014 (emmausroad.org): *Integrity Restored: Helping Catholics Win the Battle against Pornography* by Peter Kleponis, PhD.

APPENDIX TWO

Are You Called?

AN INTERVIEW WITH FATHER KYLE SCHNIPPEL, DIRECTOR OF VOCATIONS FOR THE ARCHDIOCESE OF CINCINNATI

Father Kyle Schnippel was born and raised in a Catholic family in the small town of Botkins, Ohio. After a year at Ohio State, he entered seminary formation for the Archdiocese of Cincinnati where he was ordained in 2004. After a two year stint as a teacher in a local Catholic high school, he was assigned as director of vocations where he has overseen a rise in the number of men studying for the priesthood from twenty-seven to forty-five this past year.

Father Kyle, based on your personal experience and what you have observed as the director of vocations for the Archdiocese of Cincinnati, how does a Catholic man know if he called to the diaconate, priesthood, or religious life?

"The challenge is that there is rarely one simple way to know this calling. A slogan we have used in the vocation office here in the Archdiocese of Cincinnati reflects this: 'There are rarely trumpets or midnight visions.' So many young men I talk to regarding the possibility of the priesthood desire to have that clear clarion call from God: 'Hey, you, Peter! You are being called to the priesthood!'

"Rather, I think what tends to happen more often is that there is a slow recognition of the desire to live life in a new way, to embrace the life of sacrifice and calling that the Lord is laying out before that man. There is a persistence to the calling, so that when a man is in prayer or at Mass, his thoughts start to drift towards what life would be like as a priest or a deacon. For example, he imagines what his homily would be like for that particular day.

"In the end, though, I think among most of the men that I work with (and I primarily work with men entering seminary for the priesthood, very rarely do I work with men entering formation for the permanent diaconate) is a growing dissatisfaction with the things of this world and a desire to jump deeper into the well of the Lord's Mercy as a priest."

Do you think Catholic men in today's world spend enough time in discernment and prayer to see if they have a calling to one of these vocations? Why or why not?

"I can firmly say no to this one. We (and I put myself in this camp!) get so caught up in the frenetic pace of the modern world, that to stop and spend time in prayer can be very difficult, because prayer takes discipline and patience; things that seem to be in short supply today! Also, because of the 'immediate gratification' aspects of our society, which gets fueled by that rush of social media interaction on Facebook and Twitter, we tend to lose sight of the bigger picture of where God is leading us in this world.

"Advice I often give to parents, especially parents of younger children, can be helpful here. I invite them to pray for their children (as if they don't already!), but specifically over two things: What is the unique combination of gifts and talents that God has given to each of their children? Then how is He inviting you as Mom or Dad to nourish and enrich those gifts?

"This can be a wonderful prayer experience to revisit throughout the year as well, on birthdays, Thanksgiving, Christmas, Easter, anniversaries, etc. And could also be a wonderful prayer experience for someone discerning as he recognizes those gifts God has given and seeks to share them in the appropriate setting."

What can Catholics do to promote and encourage more religious vocations for our Catholic men?

"First, among families, it is important to be respectful towards priests and religious who are in your realm. That isn't to say you cannot be critical, but to do so in a way that still respects his office. I think showing the esteem that you have for priests is a great way to encourage vocations as well, which could be as simple as making sure to celebrate the anniversary of his ordination or his birthday. Also, if you know that he does not have family in the immediate area, inviting him over for meals every once in a while, or checking in on him during holidays, can be a great way for him to interact with your family, too. Recently, a parishioner just dropped a pack of cookies at our rectory door. Having children help do such a thing is a great way to engage their imagination.

"Several parishes in my area have a traveling chalice or statue of some kind that is given to a different family each week to take home after Mass for prayer throughout the week. It can be a great way to raise awareness in the parish that vocations to the priesthood and religious life come from families just like theirs, and not just those 'super Catholic' families that we all hear about, but never actually meet.

"For older men, say out of high school or college, do not be afraid to bring up the possibility of a priestly vocation to that man you see around the parish all the time. You can certainly pray that he be open to where God is truly leading him."

What is your favorite story of a man who felt called to a religious vocation and followed through?

"It is hard to narrow it down to one single story, as I think of all the guys I have worked with during eight years in the vocation office and how each story truly is unique. A few highlights stand out for me though.

"A local parish had a very good youth minister who was doing some very good work and had a large, dynamic program going. Yet I always got the sense that there was something more going on. He had been on our radar screen since he was in high school and never wanted to be removed, so I knew something was up with him. Through a nudging from the Holy Spirit, I guess, I picked up the phone and gave him a call, just to urge him to start spiritual direction with one of the priests at the seminary which, fortunately, was just down the street from his parish. I left it with a 'let's catch up in a few months.' Well, the time passed and I called him a few months later and his response: 'Fine! I'll go to the seminary!' He will be ordained, God willing, in two years from now. You never know when a simple suggestion will pay a huge dividend!

"During my first year in the vocation office, another young man missed three appointments with me before we were ever able to connect up. I would wait for half an hour past the time we were to meet, maybe get a phone call or text that he could not make it, but would always set up another time. When he finally showed up, he was very apologetic and we talked for a good time that first night. He will be ordained a priest this coming May. Perseverance pays off!

"The common theme among all those with whom I have worked, the thing I encourage the most, is just to be open to the Spirit and to invest themselves in the process. As my Archbishop is fond of saying,

'The Lord will never be outdone in generosity,' and it continues to be proven true."

If you could address a group of Catholic men from teenagers to grandfathers, what practical advice would you share with them about remaining committed to the Church and discerning their vocation?

"There are a few aspects that I would like to touch on:

- Vocations are truly and properly discerned within the context of the Church, so stay close to her and she will lead you to where you will be happiest.
- You can never pray enough! And the fruits of that prayer can be lasting for both the individual and the parish dynamic. My home parish is fairly small, just three hundred or so families on the books in a small town of about a thousand overall folks, roughly half of whom are Catholic. When I was in the later stages of grade school and moving into high school, the parish started Eucharistic Adoration, six days a week, twenty-four hours a day. (Adoration starts after the last Mass on Sunday and runs through Friday evening.) Since that time, five men have entered seminary from that parish. Two of us are now ordained, two entered but left the seminary, and one is currently still in the seminary. Adoration and time spent before Christ in the Eucharist pays dividends in so many ways!
- A final word of encouragement: There is something powerful when men come together to pray, and in particular when fathers model prayer for their

children. It can set their children on a lifelong pursuit of the things of the kingdom, and it gives their sons a great freedom to pursue the possibility of the priesthood, because they can be assured of their father's blessing. Think of how important that was for Jacob to receive from Isaac. Are we so different?"

APPENDIX THREE

Helpful Resources for Catholic Men

HELPFUL WEBSITES

- Integrated Catholic Life eMagazine
  www.integratedcatholiclife.org
- Fathers for Good
  www.fathersforgood.org
- Knights of Columbus
  www.kofc.org
- Catholic Dads
  www.catholicdadsonline.org
- National Fellowship of Catholic Men
  www.nfcmusa.org
- The King's Men
  www.thekingsmen.org

- St. Joseph Covenant Keepers
  www.dads.org
- Crossing the Goal
  www.crossingthegoal.com
- United States Conference of Catholic Bishops
  www.usccb.org
- Priests for Life
  www.priestsforlife.org
- The Vatican
  www.vatican.va

ONLINE LEARNING RESOURCES

- Catholic Bible
  www.usccb.org/bible/
- The Catholic Encyclopedia
  www.newadvent.com
- The Catechism of the Catholic Church
  www.vatican.va/archive/ccc/index.htm
- Daily Readings
  www.usccb.org/bible/readings/012214.cfm
- The New Evangelization
  www.newevangelizers.com
- Saint of the Day
  www.americancatholic.org/features/saintofday
- *The National Catholic Register*
  www.ncregister.com

- EWTN
  www.ewtn.com
- Catholics United for the Faith
  www.cuf.org
- Catholic Answers
  www.catholic.com
- Crossroads Initiative
  www.crossroadsinitiative.com

HELP WITH PORNOGRAPHY ADDICTION

- Porn Harms
  www.pornharms.org
- *Blessed Are The Pure In Heart: A Pastoral Letter on the Dignity of the Human Person and the Dangers of Pornography* (2007) by Bishop Robert W. Finn of Kansas City-St. Joseph, Missouri. To request the booklet, visit kofc.org/cis.
- Emmaus Road Publishing's upcoming book to be released in 2014 (emmausroad.org): *Integrity Restored: Helping Catholics Win the Battle against Pornography* by Peter Kleponis, PhD.

PRAYER AND SPIRITUALITY

- The Daily Examen
  www.ignatianspirituality.com/ignatian-prayer/the-examen/

- Real Men Pray the Rosary
  www.rmptr.org
- Church Prayers and Devotions
  www.ewtn.com
- Catholic Spiritual Direction
  www.rcspiritualdirection.com

RECOMMENDED PAPAL AND CHURCH DOCUMENTS

- *Christifideles laici*: St. Pope John Paul II
- *Familiaris consortio*: St. Pope John Paul II
- *Centisimus annus*: St. Pope John Paul II
- *Fides et ratio*: St. Pope John Paul II
- *Laborem exercens*: St. Pope John Paul II
- *Caritas in veritate*: Pope Emeritus Benedict XVI
- *Evangelii gaudium:* Pope Francis
- *Lumen fidei:* Pope Francis
- *Humanae vitae:* Pope Paul VI
- Pastoral Constitution on the Church in the Modern World (*Gaudium et spes*): Second Vatican Council
- *A Catholic Framework for Economic Life*: A Statement of the U.S. Catholic Bishops**
- *How We Teach the New Evangelization***

* All papal and Church documents can be found at www.vatican.va

** These documents can be found at www.usccb.org

RECOMMENDED BOOKS

- *The Catholic Briefcase: Tools for Integrating Faith and Work* by Randy Hain
- *A Man of God: A Guide for Men* (eBook) by Fr. Roger Landry
- *Be a Man!* by Fr. Larry Richards
- *Boys to Men* by Tim Gray and Curtis Martin
- *Man to Man, Dad to Dad: Catholic Faith and Fatherhood*, edited by Brian Caulfield
- *Amazing Grace For Fathers.* by Jeff Cavins, Matthew Pinto, Mark Armstrong, and Patti Armstrong
- *Love and Responsibility* by St. Pope John Paul II
- *A Personal Relationship with Jesus* by Father Bill McCarthy, MSA